The United States and the European Union

Edited by

Gerhard Wahlers

With Contributions by

José Manuel Barroso
Elmar Brok
Benita Ferrero-Waldner
Falk-Ulrich von Hoff
Werner Langen
Angela Merkel
Hartmut Nassauer
Doris Pack
Hans-Gert Poettering
Günter Rinsche
Bernhard Vogel
Norbert Wagner
Karl von Wogau
Gerhard Wahlers

Wahlers, Gerhard., ed., *The United States and the European Union.* (Washington, DC: Konrad Adenauer Stiftung/Center for Transatlantic Relations, 2007).

Center for Transatlantic Relations
American Consortium on EU Studies
EU Center of Excellence Washington DC
The Paul H. Nitze School of Advanced
International Studies
The Johns Hopkins University
1717 Massachusetts Ave., NW, Suite 525
Washington, D.C. 20036
Tel: (202) 663-5880
Fax: (202) 663-5879
Email: transatlantic@jhu.edu
http://transatlantic.sais-jhu.edu

Konrad Adenauer Foundation
Washington Office
2005 Massachusetts Ave., NW
Washington, D.C. 20036
Tel: (202) 464-5840
Fax: (202) 464-5848
Email: office@kasusa.org

ISBN 0: 0-9788821-2-1
ISBN 13: 978-0-978821-2-9

Table of Contents

Annex: Institutions, Positions, Names, Addresses

Foreword

Bernhard Vogel

Former Minister-President of the States of Rhineland Palatinate and Thuringia
President of the Konrad Adenauer Foundation

The European Union celebrates its 50th anniversary in 2007. Exactly half a century ago, on March 25, 1957, the European Economic Community and the European Atomic Energy Community were established with the signing of the Treaties of Rome. Together with the European Coal and Steel Community that had already been created in 1952, they formed the foundation of the present day European Union.

European unification has today become a reality due to the United States and its continuous engagement with Europe over the past 60 years. Within the framework of transatlantic relations and the close partnership between the U.S. and Germany, several Americans have supported the unification of Europe as symbolic of democracy and liberty. Without this farsighted policy and the constant support of the U.S., the history of Europe in the past decades would have surely evolved very differently.

The Konrad Adenauer Foundation feels very closely connected to the success story of the European Union: without Konrad Adenauer, one of the founding fathers of the present day European Union; and without Helmut Kohl, one of the important standard-bearers of the European unification, it would not have been possible to forge so far ahead with the integration of the common market and common currency.

It was possible to overcome nationalism and war within the European Union due to European collaboration and integration. The principle underlying the collaboration among the states forming the union has remained unchanged since its inception: the states transfer a part of their sovereignty to a supranational organization, so that common problems can be resolved jointly and common interests pursued. This principle is rooted in the conviction that all partners stand to benefit more from collaboration than from isolation and mutual conflict. Conflicts, therefore, are no longer settled on the battlefield; they are resolved through negotiations across the table.

The fact that almost all states of Central and Eastern Europe wanted to join the European Union after the political change of 1989/90 demonstrates the success of the European model of integration With the accession of Romania and Bulgaria to the European Union on January 1, 2007, the EU at present has a membership of 27 states. Almost all European states have thus become members of the EU.

The enlarged EU is willing to take on greater international responsibility. We need partners for international cooperation. The U.S. and the EU have a common commitment to peace, stability, liberty and economic prosperity. Both regions are greatly interested in availing the opportunities created by globalization while at the same time confronting the perils emanating from it. The U.S. and the EU both have the common objective of combating international terrorism, containing the proliferation of weapons of mass destruction, and in resolving ethnic conflicts peacefully. In addition, the big challenges of the 21st century, such as climate protection, securing natural resources or combating global pandemics, can only be tackled and resolved jointly.

The close cooperation between the U.S. and the EU is very important in tackling potential risks of this magnitude. The relations between Europe and the U.S. are based on three pillars:

1. common values that bind us both intellectually and politically;
2. common interest in global security and stability;
3. common efforts towards establishing and maintaining a liberal and fair economic order.

These objectives shaped the collaboration between Europe and the U.S. even during the period of the Cold War. They remain as relevant today under changed circumstances as well. If we want to uphold and secure what we have thus far achieved together and also contain new risks, we must work closely together in the future too. This cooperation must be rooted in mutual confidence. We must create a global order that will reliably secure peace and freedom in the 21st century also.

Within the framework of this collaboration, the Konrad Adenauer Foundation has for a long time been holding a political dialogue with American elites. All the issues that have been discussed as part of this dialogue are extremely important. They have promoted and fostered an exchange of ideas and enhanced mutual understanding and have thus contributed to strengthening the ties of friendship between our countries.

Together with our partners, we work towards meeting political, social and economic challenges. We support reform processes and impart political education based on our Christian beliefs and ideals. We hope that one day there will be democracy, liberty, justice and prosperity all over the world.

As Chairman of the Konrad Adenauer Foundation, it gives me great pleasure to present this book, *The United States and the European Union*. It should promote a better understanding of the EU, its policies, its functioning, its institutions and its political dynamism. We are proud that so many eminent personalities of the EU, including the current President of the European Council, Chancellor Angela Merkel; President of the European Parliament, Professor Hans-Gert Pöttering MEP; President of the European Commission, Manuel Barroso; and the Commissioner for External Relations, Benita Ferrero-Waldner, have all contributed to this book. This underlines the importance of EU relations with the United States.

I hope this book will generate interest and resonance in the United States.

Preface

Angela Merkel

President of the Council of the European Union
Federal Chancellor of Germany

The European Union bears a global responsibility. Gone are the days when European policy was centered exclusively on fostering integration within Europe, with a focus on economic issues. Currently, the European Union has to increasingly address issues as a foreign policy actor in the international arena, bringing European values and interests to bear not only on issues pertaining to the global economy but also on issues concerning international security, climate protection, social standards and the respect for human rights.

The Common Foreign and Security Policy (CFSP) has given a new dimension to the evolution of external relations of the European Union. In the future, this policy area will increasingly gain in importance – not least because, in the age of globalization, individual EU member states will no longer be in a position to realize their values, goals and interests in isolation due to demographic and international economic developments.

Despite this, only a relatively small circle of experts, both within and outside of Europe, has engaged in the study of the CFSP of the European Union and its contents. I am, therefore, delighted that the Konrad Adenauer Foundation and the Center for Transatlantic Relations at Johns Hopkins University have undertaken to publish a study on *The United States and the European Union*, providing a comprehensive overview of the relations between the European Union and the United States of America, on the occasion of Germany's Presidency of the EU and of the Group of Eight (G8).

We Europeans are bound to the United States by ties of historical partnership and friendship. It is of paramount importance that both the U.S. and we Europeans continuously work towards building a transatlantic relationship rooted in confidence and trust. Our values and principles of liberty, democracy and human rights can only be defended jointly in the 21st century.

In this context, the following political areas are particularly important:

- close cooperation in the area of international economic, financial and trade relations,
- surmounting obstacles to trade,
- intensive exchange programs for youth, students and researchers,
- a continuous and close transatlantic consultative mechanism in the area of foreign and security policy,
- close cooperation between the EU and the NATO in the area of defense policy,
- close cooperation among security institutions including the Europol, FBI and intelligence agencies.

I hope this publication will be a valuable contribution in consolidating and broadening knowledge on European-American relations, and will serve to enhance the mutual understanding between Europe and America as well as provide the impetus for initiating an even more substantive dialogue between them.

Preface

Hans-Gert Poettering, MEP

President of the European Parliament

As of January 1, 2007, the European Parliament, the largest multinational parliament in the world, comprises 785 Members from 27 European states working together for the common goal of fashioning a lasting European Union based on their shared culture and history and of ensuring peace and prosperity for almost 500 million EU citizens.

As in all other democratic parliaments, most Members of the European Parliament (MEPs) belong to a political group, there being seven such groups in the current Parliament. In order to be able to form a group, at least 19 MEPs from at least six different Member States must join forces. By far the largest political group in the European Parliament is the EPP-ED group comprising Members from all 27 Member States (277 in all). National parties, which may already form part of European 'families of parties' such as the European People's Party (EPP) put forward candidates for the European Parliament. Each year, the European Parliament meets for twelve week-long part-sessions at its seat in Strasbourg and for an additional six mini part-sessions in Brussels.

The history of the European Parliament reflects the development of the European Union. Since the first direct elections in 1979, the European Parliament, whose precursor was the Common Assembly of the European Coal and Steel Community, has steadily gained additional powers. In the eighties, which represented a period of stagnation in the development of Europe, the European Parliament was still a relatively powerless institution which survived largely as a result of its creative spirit and its unshakable belief that visions can be made to come true. In 1984, in a show of enthusiasm for a united Europe, the European Parliament adopted the 'draft Treaty on the establishment of the European Union,' in effect anticipating the current Treaty establishing a Constitution for Europe.

The European Parliament wrestled for a long time with the Commission and the Council for recognition. As the only Community institution enjoying democratic legitimisation, Parliament sought to challenge the Council, particularly as regards consultation in the legislative procedure and the budget, and did not shy away from referring contentious issues to the European Court of Justice. It was only with the entry into force of the Single European Act in July 1987 that the European Parliament gained further powers: since then, Parliament's assent has been necessary for accession and association agreements. The cooperation procedure with the Council provided Parliament with the possibility for greater involvement in the legislative procedure.

The competencies of the European Parliament were further extended in 1992 with the Treaty of Maastricht. The European Parliament was granted the right to vote on the European Commission before the latter can begin its work. The most important change introduced by the Maastricht Treaty, from the point of view of the European Parliament, was without a doubt the introduction of codecision in the legislative procedure even if it was at first limited to the area of economic and monetary union. Parliament continued merely to be consulted in the areas of common foreign and security policy and justice and home affairs.

The Treaty of Amsterdam (1999) further strengthened the rights of the European Parliament. The application of the codecision principle was extended from 15 to 38 areas. In addition, Parliament has since been able to vote not just on the Commission as a whole but on the President designate put forward by the Council. The Treaty of Nice further extended codecision to cover 43 different areas. The current draft constitution places Parliament and the Council on an equal footing in approximately 90% of legislative procedures.

Today, the European Union can be proud of the fact that pressure for accession is still being exerted at its borders. This is a reflection of the economic and political success of the EU. Today's Europe, the Europe of 27, has incorporated a significant proportion of the former Soviet satellite states. The inclusion of these states, which the European Parliament always advocated, was a historical and moral imperative. These countries defeated Communism in a remarkably peaceful revolution and applied themselves with great success to the pursuit of democracy and self-determination. The new Member States always retained their Western orientation, even though for more than fifty years they were the victims of the 20th century's most ruthless and inhuman ideologies: National Socialism and Communism. They rightfully staked a claim not to be made into 'buffer' states and not to be condemned to an uncertain future in a kind of half-way house to Europe but to be included once and for all in the family of European democracies. In the words of Walter Hallstein: "There can be no stronger motive for European integration than the desire for peace." The fact that Europeans now jointly elect a Parliament every five years is perhaps the most powerful signal of reconciliation which European citizens who have waged war against each other for centuries can send.

The European Parliament has always been considered as the EU's conscience in matters of foreign policy since it make a point of focusing attention on issues such as human rights, democratic deficits, minority rights and environmental protection in the EU's external relations. Thus, at the behest of Parliament, the EU only signs cooperation agreements with third countries where a democracy clause obliges the contractual partner to protect its democratic institutions and to respect human rights. Since 1982, the European Parliament has maintained contact with third-country parliaments by means of inter-parliamentary delegations.

The European Parliament attaches a great deal of importance to improving relations between the EU and the United States of America. It has thus decided that the existing US-EU 'New Transatlantic Agenda' should be replaced with a transatlantic partnership agreement. In a resolution, the European Parliament indicated that the proposed partnership agreement should aim to establish a 'community of action for global and regional cooperation'. It has proposed involving 'parliamentary representatives and representatives from European and American civil society more fully in the day-to-day running of the partnership' and has welcomed the Transatlantic Legislators' Dialogue (TLD).

However, in describing the 'General framework of the EU-US Partnership' in 56 detailed sections, the European Parliament has also been critical of the unilateral U.S. approach, which lacks any reciprocity when dealing inter alia with EU citizens. The Guantanamo Bay Camp has also been criticised for the mistreatment of prisoners.

In view of our shared history and cultural values, there can be no alternative to a significant strengthening of the social and economic partnership with the United States. I hope that this publication will constitute an important contribution in this regard.

Preface

José Manuel Durão Barroso

President of the European Commission

In today's world there are almost no challenges facing the European Union and the United States that are not global in their origins or in their effects. With global challenges come global responsibilities. The EU and the U.S., with their shared values and common interests, make natural partners to take the lead.

There are some self-evident truths about the partnership between the EU and the U.S.: our long ties of shared history and kinship; our shared respect for freedom, democracy, human rights and the rule of law; our two-way direct investment stock worth more than €1.5 trillion; the 14 million jobs on both sides of the Atlantic which depend on our commercial ties.

Over the past years the European Union and the United States have learned useful lessons about when a common approach works, when distinct but parallel policies are most effective; and when one or the other is best placed to pursue a policy objective whilst the other gets less involved. Even in our close partnership some differences remain. But no issue is excluded from discussion and our significantly intensified dialogue at every level has clearly produced greater convergence of views and action.

But our partnership goes far beyond the usual channels of politics and business; it involves the citizens on both sides of the Atlantic, be they students and teachers, special interest groups or the millions of tourists visiting either side of the Atlantic each year. They are all part of the lively exchange of ideas that nourishes our relationship.

The benefits of our close bilateral relations reach well beyond the European Union and the United States. As powers of global significance, we have a responsibility to cooperate to provide leadership in the world which includes effective multilateral organisations. We share an outward-looking agenda and are committed to cooperating on issues of global importance. This applies as much to the field of foreign affairs and development as to the more traditional area of trade.

Publications like the one you are holding in your hands contribute not only to the taking stock of where we come from in our partnership but also where we are going. Together, the European Union and the United States can make a difference in today's world and help to resolve some of the problems facing all of us.

The United States and the European Union

EU-US Relations

Benita Ferrero-Waldner

Commissioner of Foreign Relations and Neighbourhood Policy

> *Wir leben alle unter dem gleichen Himmel, aber wir haben nicht alle den gleichen Horizont* (We all live under the same sky but we do not all have the same outlook)
>
> —Konrad Adenauer

The relationship between the United States and the European Union has come a long way since the establishment of diplomatic relations back in 1953. One might even claim that it has existed for a much longer time due to the waves of immigrants leaving Europe for the United States in the past 500 years even if the European Union was only founded in the 20th century. Ties between Europe and the United States have never been severed since. Assistance provided by the United States was crucial to re-building Europe after the nightmare of the Second World War. And after the terrorist attacks on September 11, 2001, the Europeans reconfirmed their close alliance with the United States in the fight against international terrorism.

This special relationship is based on the vast array of common values shared between the U.S. and Europe, such as democracy, the rule of law and respect for human rights and fundamental freedoms. These common values are the backbone to our indispensable partnership.

Over the years we have developed a dense network across the Atlantic closely linking our policies, economies, societies and people. Back in 1995, the EU and the United States agreed and signed the New Transatlantic Agenda, which lists four major fields for joint action: (1) promotion of peace and stability, democracy and development around the world, (2) respond to global challenges, (3) contribute to the expansion of world trade and closer economic relations and last but not least (4) building bridges across the Atlantic. This Agenda has been filled with life from our joint efforts in securing peace and stability for instance in the Balkans to the promotion of innovative cooperation projects between EU and U.S. educational institutions.

In a speech given in February 2006 at Georgetown University, President Barroso said, “Europe needs the U.S. and the U.S. needs Europe. When we speak with a common voice, no challenge is too great. When we speak with a common voice, we are truly an indispensable partnership.” This is especially true with regard to the numerous challenges we are facing in the field of foreign affairs. There has been a steady increase in the depth and breadth of the transatlantic foreign policy cooperation.

At the 2005 EU-U.S. Summit both sides spelled out their commitment, which serves as guideline for cooperation in foreign policy: “The EU and the U.S. believe that the spread of accountable and representative government, the rule of law, and respect for human rights as enshrined in the Universal Declaration of Human Rights, are a strategic priority as well as a moral necessity. We will continue to work together to advance these priorities around the world.”

An evident example is our joint engagement in the Balkans. Following the conclusion of the Dayton peace agreement in 1995 the EU and the U.S. have worked alongside in providing humanitarian and emergency aid, including reconstruction activities. We also fostered political reconciliation and facilitated the return of refugees. The EU’s stabilization and association process not only provides assistance and encourages reforms but it also creates a framework that can lead to eventual EU membership. Today the peace-keeping mission in Bosnia is the largest operation launched by the EU.

Afghanistan is another impressive example for the close cooperation between the EU and the U.S., given that we both are the principal providers of aid and reconstruction assistance to the country. Between 2004 and 2006 the EU committed € 2.2 billion to this end. Several EU-Member States provide troops the UN forces (ISAF) and to the U.S.-led Operation Enduring Freedom that is continuing anti-terrorist operations.

Perhaps less prominent but equally important are our efforts to assist Africa’s governments in fighting poverty, disease, corruption and internal or cross-border conflicts. 55% of overseas development aid to sub-Saharan Africa is provided by the EU and its Member States. At the same time the EU and the U.S. are committed to strengthening the capacity of regional bodies such as the African Union and to encouraging regional economic integration.

Peace and stability in the Middle East are a goal the EU and the U.S. work for not only within the Middle East Quartet (together with Russia and the United Nations). Through the Temporary International Mechanism, developed and managed by the European Commission, financial support is provided to alleviate the civilian hardship in the Palestinian Territories and to purchase fuel to power generators for hospitals and water plants in Gaza to name just two examples.

Multilateralism is at the core of EU foreign policy. When the EU and the U.S. are acting united, they can be more persuasive in convincing other countries to develop common solutions and approaches, in line with shared values, to the many serious issues facing the global community. Effective multilateral organisations are in the interest of all of us. Therefore, the EU and the U.S. are actively engaged in the reform process of the United Nations to make sure that the structures and procedures of this crucial multilateral organisation are up to handling the challenges of today and of the future.

Nevertheless, like all partners, the EU and the U.S. do not always agree, but in most instances these disagreements are about tactics rather than the values that underpin our ongoing association. A close network of formal and informal contacts helps to identify and in most cases solve such issues.

Basic differences persist for example on the question of the death penalty. The European Union is opposed to the death penalty in all cases and in all countries. This position is rooted in the inherent dignity of all human beings and the inviolability of the human person, regardless of the crime committed. Therefore, the EU does not extradite any individual to a country where the death penalty could be imposed for the crime being alleged.

Today, we have a tendency of underestimating the extent to which the transatlantic partnership touches our daily lives. Together the EU and the U,S, represent 10% of the world's population and account for approximately 40% of world trade. The U.S.-EU economic relationship dwarfs America's economic ties with China. European investment in Texas alone exceeds all U.S. investment in China and Japan put together. About 14 million jobs on both sides of the Atlantic depend on our economic relationship.

But let's not get carried away by these impressive figures, which give an indication of how closely our economies are integrated. The U.S. and the EU also remain competitors in today's global markets. Different regulatory systems and approaches may be causes for problems and potential trade disputes. It is important to note that the economic impact of these disputes constitutes less that 2% of overall bilateral trade. However, it is those trade issues such as hormones, genetically modified organisms and subsidies for large civil aircraft industries that make the headlines.

At the same time, the EU and the U.S. often work together in developing international standards including the liberalization of trade, combating of piracy and intellectual property violations. A wide array of mechanisms has been developed over the past years to manage these questions. The 2005 EU-US Summit launched the "EU-U.S. initiative to enhance transatlantic economic integration and growth." This initiative covers a wide array of areas including regulatory cooperation, capital markets, trade and transport security, competition, investment and intellectual property rights to name just a few. A joint detailed work programme endorsed by the first ever EU-U.S. informal economic ministerial meeting in 2005 identifies the steps both sides intend to take in order to reach closer economic integration.

Recent events reminded us all of the need to secure the supply of energy on the long run. This is another challenge we can solve only at international level. With global demand for oil and gas growing rapidly, oil dependence is a great concern not only for the EU. At the June 2006 summit the EU and the U.S. agreed to establish a "High Level Dialogue on Climate Change, Clean Energy and Sustainable Development," which identified a number of areas for joint activities during its first meeting. The EU and the U.S. will cooperate in the commercial deployment of clean coal and carbon sequestration technologies, in research and development of second-generation biofuels, on international standards on the use and trade of other renewable energy sources, on energy efficiency actions across various sectors and on coordinating actions on combating the loss of biodiversity.

The threat of global terrorism has demonstrated the depth of transatlantic shared values and interests like no other issue since the Cold War. EU-U.S. cooperation in this field has been robust and continues to grow stronger.

In 2004 more than 45 million air passengers travelled between an EU-25 country and the United States. In addition, 2.41 million tons of freight and mail were transported by air during the same year. Thus it is obvious that cooperation in the area transport security for air and sea transportation is important to us. Improvements include the expansion of customs cooperation to cover container security and the agreement on the transfer of passenger name records. The development and introduction of secure passports incorporating biometric data is another area on which the EU and the U.S. consulted closely. Finally, measures by the EU and the U.S. to cut off financing of terrorist activities have been strengthened, for instance by increased scrutiny of wire transfers and cross-border cash movements.

The picture of the broad and colourful relationship between the European Union and the United States would be incomplete if it forgot to add the color provided by the numerous links between people on either side of the Atlantic. Most of these links exist and flourish without the need for active involvement by the political level, for example the thousands of pupils and students who spend a year or even longer attending classes at schools or universities in either the U.S. or Europe. In other areas, such as the cooperation of universities and research institutions, governments and the European Commission can be helpful in kick-starting the process. Today, there are 10 EU Centers of Excellence at U.S. universities, supported by the EU Commission in recognition of the high quality, variety and depth of their EU studies activities. These centres promote the study of the EU and EU-U.S. relations through teaching programs, scholarly research and outreach activities in their local and regional communities.

Transatlantic relations touch literally every aspect of our lives on both sides of the Atlantic. Even though this relationship is based on a solid foundation of common values, it needs to be nurtured continuously. The ultimate goal is to optimize it, making it even more fruitful and mutually beneficial, to increase prosperity and well-being on both sides of the Atlantic, and to enable the EU and the U.S. to contribute to increased global security, stability and prosperity.

Stability and Efficiency: Common Perspectives and Requirements in the Era of Globalization

Günter Rinsche

Member of the Board of the Konrad Adenauer Foundation

Fifty years ago, on May 17, 1957, the German Federal Chancellor and Founding Father of the European Community, Konrad Adenauer, had highlighted the need for global development in a conversation with Nobel Prize winner Arthur H. Compton. Adenauer said: "Our enemies of today are not other nations. Our enemies are poverty, ignorance, diseases and discrimination. What we need is a co-operation based on the idea that the entire world is one human family. Ignorance and lack of understanding among nations is the greatest danger we are facing today."

Around 200 years ago the philosopher Voltaire (1694–1788) stated that "the prosperity of nations is based on the freedom of thinking and of trade." At the same time the French political thinker Montesquieu (1689–1755) wrote: "The history of trade is the history of international understanding."

In 1917, 90 years ago, during the First World War, Oswald Spengler, a German historian, published a book entitled "The Decline of the West."

On December 19, 1946, when wide stretches of Europe did indeed resemble a moonscape or a graveyard, Winston Churchill said in Zurich: "A dissonant Babylonian confusion of languages prevails among the victors, as the solemn silence of despair prevails among the vanquished". And he went on to say: "Yet there is a remedy. What is this cure-all? Simply to raise the family of Europe, or as many of its members as possible, up form the dust, and give it a constitution under which it may live in peace, security and freedom. We must create a kind of United States of Europe."

The vision of the British statesman was seized upon and translated into practical politics by great European statesmen including Robert Schuman, the French Foreign Minister, Alcide de Gasperi, the Italian Prime Minister, and Konrad Adenauer, the German Federal Chancellor.

In the first half of 20th century, Europe witnessed two terrible world wars that had originated from European disputes and totalitarian ideologies: the dictatorships of Hitler and Stalin; the fateful division of Germany and Europe. All of which resulted in immeasurable pain, suffering, misery, enslavement, and insecurity.

The second half of the 20th century saw the unification of Western Europe, the reconciliation of nations, reconstruction based on democracy and social market economy and, ultimately, the reunification of Germany and Europe. These events heralded a fascinating opportunity of establishing an all-European order based on freedom, peace, and human rights.

The integration of Europe is a success story. Imperfections and unsolved problems notwithstanding, the European Union acquired a magnetic hold over millions of people and became a model of peaceful togetherness among nations. When compared to other times and other countries, the political achievements of European integration stand out.

But achievements alone cannot guarantee success in the future, for nations may be led into the so-called success trap. There is no permanent guarantee on the prosperity and stability of the European Union.

Now in Europe and in the United States we are facing the problems of globalization. The responsible leaders and managers in politics, economy and society are facing a new state of affairs. In other words, globalisation represents an age of change, chance and challenge.

Responsible people have to deal with rapidly changing structures, problems, facts and basic data. They have to make use of the new chances. Last but not least, they have to respond to the global challenges in the correct manner in a timely fashion.

These assignments are likewise indispensable in the United States and the European Union. Therefore it is reasonable to discuss the problems and to cooperate in solving them. Two central questions must be answered before any action is taken. They are:

What do our people want?

What is globalization?

Human beings want security and prosperity. Security means peace, the rule of law and political stability. The prerequisites for prosperity are socioeconomic growth, social responsibility and efficiency.

The term "globalization" has become a buzzword in the public debate. There are many people who fear globalization. Besides, many in Europe are afraid that their social status might be undermined by competitors from beyond their borders. There are calls for global minimum standards in environmental protection and human rights; and for minimum wages for employees, so as to keep cheap imports from developing countries in check. The developing countries, in turn, are afraid of being 'ruled by international capital owners' and concerned about the unpredictability of international financial transactions and their consequences for their own economic and social situation.

There is no doubt that there are many important questions relating to globalisation to which the right answers have yet to be found. The only way of doing this is through international co-operation among partners of equal standing. We must inform each other of the realities of globalisation, and we must agree on its opportunities and requirements. Only when we have succeeded in creating an efficient system of international cooperation, will we be able to overcome the problems of globalisation and exploit its opportunities for the benefit of all.

The Konrad Adenauer Foundation regards these facts as an important mandate. It is our goal to contribute towards promoting mutual appreciation and understanding, the exchange of information, and the efficiency of global cooperation through international encounters of persons in positions of political, cultural and economic responsibility, as well as through seminars, discussions, and publications. As such, the foundation constantly strives to have an unprejudiced perception of reality.

Globalization is the Reality of the 21th Century

Globalization is characterised by

1. Global transparency through, for instance, more than a thousand million television sets worldwide and, more importantly, the rapidly increasing number of Internet users;

2. Swift communication through, for instance, communication satellites, facsimile transmissions, e-mail, etc.; and

3. Worldwide systems of fast transport including, for instance, a network of airlines operating large jet aircraft, high-speed trains, many millions of passenger cars, container technologies, etc.

The forces that control and power globalization, i.e. its factors and motors, include:

1. the rapid decline of transport and communication costs;

2. supra-national integration (e.g. the EU, ASEAN, etc.), the strengthening of multi-national trade regulations (e. g. the WTO), and the gradual elimination of political tension (e.g. through the end of the Cold War between the Western powers and the Soviet bloc);

3. the adaptation of development strategies and the liberalization of foreign trade policies in numerous newly-industrialised and developing countries; and

4. the emergence of India and China in the world market and in the international system of labour division.

Furthermore, the following development trends and effects of globalization are also equally notable:

In Europe, electronic mail or e-mail, one of the major elements of Internet use, has already outgrown the volume of traditional postal services. In so doing, it is revolutionising communication worldwide. The worldwide web (www), a universally-accessible system for conveying all kinds of information, allows all its users to gather and transmit information worldwide at relatively low expense. As far as the exchange of information and the acquisition of knowledge and know how is concerned, the world is now without boundaries. The worldwide telework is becoming one of the reasons for globalization.

Globalization alters the economic field by heightening the worldwide labour divisions. One of the consequences of this is the break-up of multi-stage production processes into fragments, which are then distributed over various production locations. This has led to a swift expansion of the international goods trade and foreign direct investment, as well as to the growing integration of capital markets worldwide. This, in turn, causes interdependencies to arise among markets and production processes. For this reason, the internationalization of the economic processes may be regarded as the salient characteristic of globalization. Another remarkable point is the increasing adaptation of national and local demand and consumption structures, a tendency which is particularly apt to influence the situation and development of small and medium-sized enterprises.

There is no blanket answer to the question of whether the developing countries are victims or beneficiaries of globalization. Thanks to the technological progress described above, the mobility of many production factors is growing, while their affinity to particular locations is declining. This makes for increasing competition among locations, regions, and countries.

Next to foreign direct investment (a factor of great importance to the developing countries), the volume of capital transfers in the form of bonds, bank loans, and share purchases has also increased enormously. The net flow of capital into the developing countries (with the exception of most African states) tripled between 1990 and 1996, increasing to $97 billion. However, short-term capital is highly volatile and may be withdrawn surprisingly and at very short notice if the general situation were to become uncertain. This represents a grave risk for any borrower. The dangers associated with this risk showed up very clearly in the Asian Financial crisis of Thailand, Korea, and Indonesia.

Yet the advantages of world trade growth are indisputable, as the international division of labour enhances efficiency. Better efficiency is tantamount to economic growth, which could be advantageous to all, provided that discrimination is avoided. This holds true also for direct investment that includes knowledge and technological know-how in the transfer of capital.

As previously mentioned, some difficulties and dangers might result from the volatility and uncertainty of short-term capital flows. The instability which this engenders on the financial markets, particularly in the developing and newly-industrialized countries, is especially dangerous wherever unstable, inefficient, and defective national banking systems and financial infrastructures are involved.

In their turn, the developing countries are confronted by the question of how they respond to globalisation. Globalization implies participation in world trade, as well as active global competition. Any attempt to shy off from this competition by, for instance, avoiding any contact with world trade in the manner practised by North Korea, would merely lead to mass poverty. One should also embrace technological progress. Indeed, the ruling maxim is 'One cannot unlearn,' meaning one cannot turn the wheel of knowledge backward. Avoiding contact with world trade was attempted in the early 1930s by both in the U.S. and Europe, where beggar-my-neighbour policies were implemented, resulting in mass destitution and total war.

If we assume that the dictates of reason are followed, discrimination is avoided, and productive partnership promoted in politics, global economy is not a zero-sum game in which winning is possible only at the expense of another. Rather, it represents a fascinating opportunity:

- to ensure sustainable development on all continents,
- to facilitate individual opportunities and improve the quality of life,
- to optimise value creation and minimize resource consumption,
- to improve the quality of the environment worldwide, and
- to cooperate globally on solving mankind's most important problems.

Using the opportunities offered by globalization is vital, because the alternatives of worldwide co-operation would be chaos, anarchy, mass migration and the displacement of entire nations.

Thus, the basic rule of globalization is this: a bigger cake should be baked so that everyone may have a slice of it and the latecomers would not be left fighting over crumbs. The European Community's economic history of the last forty years sought to do exactly this.

Indeed, Adam Smith, the father of modern economics, wrote in his book *An Inquiry into the Nature and Causes of the Wealth of Nations*, "A prosperous man will probably be a better customer for the industrious people in his neighbourhood than a poor man, and exactly the same holds true for a rich country."

That international trade promotes affluence had already been pointed out by Adam Smith's friend, the English political philosopher David Hume, who said, "Wherever there is free exchange among nations, the progress of one must serve to support another in the domestic economy of each."

Nevertheless, it must be quite clear, that globalization requires political management and by extension, international cooperation. The German Federal President, Horst Köhler, in his former function as Director General of the International Monetary Fund, set out five guide posts for the IMF in its contribution toward a better globalization:

- **First,** issues of international *interdependence* must be given greater priority in national policy agendas. To increase mutual dependence, each country must give more consideration to the consequences of its actions on others. That in turn requires closer international cooperation and institutions directly responsible for global problems;

- **Second,** globalization urgently requires international solidarity. **Solidarity** is, however, not just an ethical and moral duty. In actively combating world poverty, we are investing in stability and peace for the whole of mankind.

- **Third,** international cooperation and solidarity should not weaken or even replace national *self-responsibility.* At the end of the day, good governance, sound institutions, and respect for the rule of law are central to each state;

- **Fourth,** the market economy has proven to be the best mechanism for economic coordination. Nevertheless, market forces alone are not sufficient. We need internationally recognized *ground rules* for participation in globalization.

- **Fifth,** we should regard the *diversity* of experiences and cultures as part of the wealth of our planet. Strengthening the international financial architecture should not therefore be an attempt to force all countries into a uniform, one-size-fits-all economic or cultural model.

These guiding-principles could be used to strengthen stability and efficiency as common requirements of the United States and the European Union in the era of globalization. So let me conclude by quoting Jacques Delors, former president of the EU-Commission:

> *Competition stimulates us, Co-operation strengthens us,*
> *Solidarity unites us!*"

The Evolution and Tasks of the Delegations of the European Parliament

Hartmut Nassauer

Member of the European Parliament (MEP)

The European Parliament, like all other parliaments, organizes its work within committees, which in conformity with the competencies and procedures laid down in the European Treaties, have been entrusted with preparatory work, especially on legislative procedures, to facilitate decision-making in the plenary sessions. In addition to this, the European Parliament has created another instrument in the form of its inter-parliamentary delegations, which in particular reflect the multifaceted relations of the European Parliament with other countries, both European and non-European. Inter-parliamentary delegations interact with parliamentary bodies of other countries, partly on the basis of agreements concluded by the EU with non-member states. The delegations may be classified as follows:

1. Joint Parliamentary Committees are based on association agreements of the EU with third countries. These form the parliamentary pillar alongside the corresponding government committees. Joint Parliamentary Committees exist, above all, between the European Parliament and countries that have applied for membership of the EU.

2. Parliamentary Cooperation Committees also formally exist within the framework of partnership and cooperation agreements signed between the EU and third countries. They reflect the parliamentary involvement in the follow-up to partnership and cooperation agreements.

3. The conventional delegations promote and maintain parliamentary contacts between the EU and other countries, both

European and non-European. These delegations are instituted either by parliament itself and/or are the result of specific agreements signed between the EU and other states.

4. The European Parliament also sends delegations to other inter-parliamentary assemblies such as the Parliamentary Assembly of the African, Caribbean and Pacific countries (ACP) and also of the NATO.

5. Finally, mention must be made of the so-called ad hoc delegations that are set up by the Conference of Presidents in response to particular events and for specific purposes. Thus, for example, ad hoc delegations visited the Kurdish areas in Iran and Turkey to assure themselves of alleged human rights violations. In the Gulf too, a European Parliament (EP) ad hoc delegation reported on the consequences of the Iraqi invasion of Kuwait. Ad hoc delegations of the European Parliament are often deputed as election observers, particularly to places where free elections are being held for the first time. Since 1989, more than 50 EP delegations have been dispatched all over the world to observe elections with a view to studying on the spot compliance with the rule of law and democratic norms.

Historical Evolution

The oldest Joint Parliamentary Committee of the European Union is that with Turkey. It was set up in the 1960s, following the signing of the Association Agreement in 1963 between the European Economic Community and Turkey. In 1972, an inter-parliamentary delegation with the United States of America was created. The number of delegations increased rapidly after the first direct elections to the European Parliament in 1979, and in 1989, at the end of the second parliamentary term of the European Parliament, the number of delegations had already risen to 27.

The reasons for setting up delegations have varied considerably. The delegations for relations with the Maghreb and Mashreq countries and also with Israel emerged from the relevant agreements signed between the EU and the concerned countries. The role of these delegations was to promote the requisite relations and contacts through parliamentary channels also. In other cases, third countries themselves requested that parliamentary relations be established with the expanding European Union because they believed such contacts were desirable. Occasionally countries whose own democratic structures were dubious sought to establish relations with the European Parliament in the hope of acquiring parliamentary credentials through their association with the European Parliament.

The 1990s saw a sudden spurt in the number of Joint Parliamentary Committees in the wake of the EU enlargement. Austria, Cyprus and Malta were accorded this status after they applied for membership to the EU. The relations of the European Parliament with Finland, Norway and Sweden followed a similar track subsequent to the acceptance of their candidature by the European Commission. These Joint Parliamentary Committees met relatively frequently and remained associated with the ongoing negotiations by making parliamentary statements. Their role came to an end with the accession of the partner countries to the EU. A similar process was followed in the second half of nineties of the previous century, when Joint Parliamentary Committees were set up with the candidate countries, which became members of the European Union on May 1, 2004.

The new form of the Parliamentary Cooperation Committees emerged from the agreements that the European Union concluded with a series of countries of the former Soviet Union. These Committees are responsible for maintaining relations with Russia, Ukraine, Moldova, Armenia, Azerbaijan, Georgia, Kazakhstan, Kyrgyzstan and Uzbekistan.

Composition and Functioning

At of January 2007 there are 32 delegations in the European Parliament (see list in appendix).

They are set up in the same way as parliamentary committees at the beginning of a parliamentary term. It is the parliamentary plenary that decides on the setting up of delegations as well as on the number of its members on the recommendation of Conference of the Presidents. The delegations should reflect the power relations in parliament, even if the composition of the delegation is not a mathematically accurate reflection thereof. The guiding principle enshrined in the relevant Rule of Procedure (Rule 188 Para 2) stipulates that "as far as possible a fair representation of Member States and political views" should be ensured.

The number of members of delegations varies greatly. Currently, including substitute members, the membership of delegations varies from 16 (Moldova) to 131 (Joint Parliamentary Assembly, ACP-EU based on parity). The size of delegations is occasionally the subject matter of internal discussions. In principle, every Member of Parliament should have the opportunity to work in a delegation as a full member. However, after the accession of new member states on May 1, 2004 and the concomitant increase in parliament seats to 732, it became necessary to restrict the size of the delegations. One reason for this was the expenditure linked to the work of the delegations; another was evidence pointing to the efficacy of visits to partner countries, if the delegation was not too large. Smaller visiting delegations are more efficient, mobile, able to interact better and less liable to attract the attention of a highly critical public as indulging themselves in irresponsible parliamentary tourism. On the other hand, equally important is the fact that some partner countries view the size of the delegation as reflecting the importance accorded to them by the EU. The size and the function of the delegation have to be finely balanced, requiring immense care.

The delegation is led by a chairman and two vice chairmen, who, according to the Rules of Procedure of the European Parliament, have to be elected by the delegations. Despite this rule, in practice the executive positions of the delegation reflect the strength of the political groups in the European Parliament and are allocated according to the d'Hondt method. Consequently, the political groups in the delegations propose the chairpersons and vice-chairpersons. As a rule, the members of the delegations accept these proposals. Occasionally there is a conflict of interests, as when a proposal that is routinely accepted meets with political resistance. Thus, for example, in the second half of the 1990s, the Canadian Parliament refused cooperation with the EP delegation. In this case, the Chairman of the delegation was a French parliamentarian, who publicly supported the independence of the Canadian province of Quebec. Since the European Parliament was not prepared to entertain an objection by another Parliament regarding its internal decision on the chairmanship of a delegation, parliamentary relations with the Canadian Parliament remained suspended until such time as fresh elections took place as scheduled and a new chairperson took office.

Tasks and Functioning of the Inter-Parliamentary Delegations

Over time the tasks of the inter-parliamentary delegations have become very diverse. The primary task, however, remains the fostering of mutual understanding. Within their geographical jurisdiction as well as within the framework of their treaty obligations, all delegations have the duty of maintaining a continuous dialogue and network of contacts with parliaments with whom the European Union has relations. This means fulfilling procedural obligations laid down in agreements in connection with accession negotiations as also an informal exchange of views and information on political developments. This also includes parliamentary support for the foreign policy aspirations of the European Union. In principle this implies that external relations should not be a monopoly of the European Commission and the Council and should in fact be imbued with the vision and spirit of parliament. Finally, it is the task of the members of the delegation to provide information about their partner countries to the European Parliament on issues ranging from the development and expansion of EU economic relations to evaluating the human rights situation.

The European Parliament has increasingly focused with great intensity on the latter aspect, which has often led to friction with partner countries. But success has equally been achieved in this difficult area. In 1991, a delegation of the European Parliament succeeded for the first time in obtaining permission to visit Tibet and to address the issue of human rights violations. It was because of the pressure applied by the delegation for relations with the Central Asian Republics that the Partnership and Cooperation Agreement with Uzbekistan was suspended for eighteen months due to the problematic human rights situation in the country. The delegation insisted on changes being introduced before Parliament gave the green light for the resumption of negotiations in March 1999.

At the same time, there is no denying the fact that the European Parliaments' human rights debate has evoked a mixed reaction. In Asian countries in particular, any references by the European Parliament to a violation of human rights or to deficient democratic and legal structures are dismissed as interference in the internal affairs of a country. The concept of Asian values is brandished to counter European demands for freedom of religion, democratic liberties and the guaranteeing of the rule of law. In this connection, the notion of the collective being privileged over the individual in Asia is emphasized. However, the European Parliament has no other option but to speak out in favor of its perception of human rights and democratic liberties, even in its relations with partner countries. Nevertheless, it has on occasion been demonstrated that the very fundamental resolutions passed by the European Parliament in Strasburg would not always survive the harsh political realities of the country against which the resolution is directed. Experience till date has shown that the European Parliament must restrain itself from pointing fingers, and accommodation in human rights issues, especially when it concerns the fate of an individual, is more likely to be achieved through diplomatic channels than through widely resounding public declarations. In the context of human rights issues also, the work of the European Parliament delegations has been most successful when public pressure has appropriately been combined with diplomatic skill and finesse.

The gradual evolution of foreign policy positions of the EU has opened up a new area of work for the delegations. Irrespective of the fact that the parliamentary role in foreign policy is located in the Foreign Affairs Committee of Parliament, the delegations of the European Parliament do have an advantage due to their knowledge of their partner countries that can benefit foreign policy makers also. This is one reason why delegations present a report on their visits before the Foreign Affairs Committee. The inception of the diplomatic service as provided for in the European Constitutional Treaty, *will* once again result in a shift in balance in external relations – this time from the Missions of individual Member States to the EU Mission. The present arrangement, that occasionally annoys partner countries, is the coexistence of Embassies of the Member States and the Delegation of the European Commission, which is responsible for the external relations of the European Union. The growing significance of European foreign policy is reflected in the growing importance of the EP delegations, which would then have the unique opportunity to utilize their knowledge and ties to their partner countries in the formulation of foreign policy *vis-à-vis* the partner countries.

In this way the delegations are not only ambassadors of the European Union in the partner countries, but they also have the opportunity to promote the positions taken by the European Union as well to garner support for the European Union itself i.e. for the idea of European integration and for the understanding of the emergence of an *European* entity. There is growing interest in acquiring information on this European development, particularly in regions of this planet where considerable thought is being given to governmental cooperation.

European Integration as a Model

European integration as a model has a special significance for the ASEAN states. Since several years, there has been a fruitful and productive exchange of views on economic relations, human rights issues and political problems in general, with this region. The ASEAN countries are increasingly interested in obtaining precise information on the basics of European integration. They are also interested in assessing how far European integration can serve as a model for their own aspirations at cooperation. The reason for this is that European integration increasingly symbolizes a successful attempt at regional cooperation. This view is linked to the emergence of a self-confident European Union, which is acquiring political weight alongside its member states, a fact that is reflected in political appraisals in the ASEAN countries. The enlargement of the European Union by ten new member states on May 1, 2004 has dramatically highlighted this development. Due to this enlargement, the European Union has finally gone beyond being a regional alliance and now represents virtually the whole of Europe – more so than it has ever done before. The expansion of the European internal market, resulting from the enlargement, is being followed closely in Asia. Even prior to the enlargement, the experiment of a single currency was followed with utmost attention. The initial skepticism in the ASEAN countries, which was spurred on by those backing the dollar has since given place to the conviction that the euro is well on its way to becoming the second global reserve currency. The successful introduction of the euro is a further reason for the ASEAN countries to examine the model character of the European example.

This issue is steadily gaining in importance within the agenda of the ASEAN delegation of the European Parliament. At all meetings with ASEAN representatives, parliamentarians, government representatives, economists and scientists, in the ASEAN countries or during the visits of the ASEAN delegation to Europe, the "Report on European Developments" is always included in the agenda. In this context, in the recent past, the developments towards a European Constitutional Treaty, enlargement and the debate on the boarders of the European Union as well as the possible membership of Turkey and the fluctuations of the euro have all been closely examined. There is an increasing understanding of the distinction made by Europeans between inter-governmental cooperation and an integrative approach. In discussions with ASEAN representatives, particularly with parliamentarians, it quickly becomes clear that closer governmental cooperation in the ASEAN region, at least for the foreseeable future, can only be envisaged in terms of inter-governmental cooperation. From the perspective of the ASEAN countries, the European experience does not throw much light on the emergence of a supra-national community. One reason for this is that the geographical location of the ASEAN countries as compared to that of the European countries is not conducive to promoting cooperation as indispensable. The historical reasons for European integration also cannot be applied to the ASEAN countries. The corollary to this is, that the inter-governmental approach is increasingly being pursued. In the meantime, ASEAN has begun signing trade agreements. The idea of a common market, or at least a free trade zone, is increasingly gaining ground. Occasionally parliamentary colleagues from the ASEAN countries do ponder the possibility of introducing a common currency, but it is clear to them that a common currency presupposes not only the existence of a common market but also of a common political foundation.

The exchange of views between the EP ASEAN delegation with the parliamentarians of the ASEAN countries at bilateral meetings and especially at the annual conference of the ASEAN parliamentarians in the AIPO played a very productive role in deliberating on the issue of how the ASEAN countries could achieve closer governmental cooperation. The interaction with parliamentarians of the ASEAN countries is not restricted to merely providing information that is required; it also serves to strengthen the importance of parliamentarism itself. Delegations maintain regular contacts with government representatives but their real partners are, however, members of parliament. Parliaments and parliamentarians in all partner countries do not play as important a role, even constitutionally, as they do in Europe. Sensitive and self-confident European members of parliament are, therefore, certainly in a position to extend support and encouragement to parliamentarians striving for recognition and political importance. Parliamentarianism backed by independent, strong parliaments is everywhere in the world the basis for democracy, rule of law and liberty. The delegations of the European Parliament have the opportunity, often under difficult conditions, to advance this process step by step.

Appendix: European Parliamentary Delegations

1. EU-Croatia
2. EU-Former Yugoslav Republic of Macedonia
3. EU-Turkey
4. EU- Mexico
5. EU-Chile
6. Switzerland, Iceland and Norway and European Economic Area
7. South-East Europe
8. Russia
9. Ukraine
10. Moldova
11. Belarus
12. Kazakhstan, Kyrgyzstan, Uzbekistan, Tajikistan, Turkmenistan and Mongolia
13. Armenia, Azerbaijan and Georgia
14. Israel
15. Palestinian Legislative Council
16. Maghreb
17. Mashreq
18. Gulf States, Yemen
19. Iran
21. United States of America
22. Canada
23. Central America
24. Andean Community
25. Mercosur
26. Japan
27. Peoples Republic of China
28. South Asia, SAARC
29. South East Asia, ASEAN
30. Korean Peninsula
31. Australia and New Zealand
33. South Africa
33. NATO

The Impact of the German CDU/CSU Delegation in the European Parliament

Werner Langen, MEP

Head of the German CDU/CSU Delegation in the European Parliament

Since the European elections in 2004 the German CDU and CSU are represented by 49 out of a total of 99 German members of the European Parliament in Brussels and Strasbourg. For the second time after the 1999 elections, the CDU/CSU is therefore the biggest national delegation not only in the EPP-ED Group but also within the European Parliament as a whole. There are more Christian Democratic members of parliament than German socialists, communists and greens together. Therefore the CDU/CSU delegation needs to fulfil its special obligation to implement Christian Democratic aims in European politics. The German CDU/CSU members have to meet the additional expectation of securing a political balance within the EPP-ED Group. Hans-Gert Poettering represents this special responsibility since his election to chairman of the EPP-ED Group in 1999. The special role of the German delegation and their party leader Angela Merkel was also shown when the president of the European Commission, José Durao Barroso, was nominated by the CDU/CSU. This influence has also played a central role in the election of a new president of the European Parliament in January 2007, with Hans-Gert Poettering elected as the candidate of the EPP-ED Group.

In contrast to the European Commission and the Council, the European Parliament is the only European institution which fully meets in public. In particular the co-decision procedure in second reading gives the European Parliament an important role in the legislative process. Because changes to draft legislation in second reading require a qualified majority in the plenary, there is a need for cooperation amongst the two biggest political groups. This has been a common procedure before a "grand coalition" was even discussed in Germany. Indeed, during several important legislative procedures in the past, it was an agreement between the Christian democrats and the socialists which paved the way for a broad majority in the final plenary vote, leading to a strong position of the European Parliament in relation to the Council. The decisions in 2006 on the services directive or the new chemicals policy "REACH" are just two examples where a "grand coalition" in the European Parliament could overcome both blockades in the Council and special national interests. In both cases, a good compromise was found, in many ways negotiated and influenced by the CDU/CSU Delegation.

The cooperation of CDU and CSU in a parliamentary unit has been successfully implemented in both the European Parliament and the German Bundestag. The cooperation with the German Bundestag and a direct contact with the executive were improved by the election of the new German government under the leadership of Chancellor Angela Merkel in 2005.

This political cooperation is necessary if European legislative processes have to be coordinated with German interests and Christian democratic views. If the CDU/CSU Delegation can communicate and influence the most important issues before final decisions are being taken at EU level, this also facilitates the implementation of European decisions into national law. The representation of members of the CDU/CSU Delegation in the national executive of both CDU and CSU is an expression of this intense cooperation.

The influence of the CDU/CSU Delegation is further reflected by the fact that 18 of its members are also represented in the Bureau of the EPP-ED Group. In the European

Parliament as a whole, in each of the 24 parliamentary committees, the CDU/CSU Delegation is represented by at least one full member and a substitute member. The same is true of the 35 delegations of the European Parliament, and especially the Interparliamentary Delegations for relations with countries outside the European Union that have not applied for membership.

The CDU/CSU Delegation supports the intense dialogue with the U.S., South America and Asia. The ASEAN Delegation of the European Parliament, chaired by a German CDU member, works together both with the Association of Southeast Asian Nations (ASEAN) as a whole as well as its member countries Indonesia, Malaysia, the Philippines, Singapore, Thailand, Brunei, Vietnam, Laos, Myanmar and Cambodia.

In the SAARC (Southasia) Delegation of the European Parliament four CDU/CSU members work towards a good exchange of views with India, Nepal, Sri Lanka, Bangladesh, Bhutan and the Maldives. There is also a delegation of the European Parliament for relations with China, which deals, amongst others, with important issues related to economic and energy aspects. At the same time the European Parliament maintains good relations with parliamentarians from the United States, Mercosur, Andean Community and Central America, both delegations being supported by CDU and CSU members.

The current legislative period is dominated by the discussion on the future of Europe. 50 years of European unity will be celebrated in 2007 with the anniversary of the treaties of Rome. This model of integration —established in large parts by Christian democratic politicians— brought freedom, peace and welfare to the countries of the EU. Today, the euro, a Europe without borders, and the single market are achievements which are universally accepted. These developments wield enormous influence and attraction for many countries neighbouring the EU. Many of them want to become members of the EU or at least develop a very close relationship with the union. But the Europe of the founding fathers Schuman, de Gasperi and Adenauer has to be modified so that it can cope with the challenges of the 21st century.

It is the constitutional treaty that forms the basis for more effective working procedures and the further development of an enlarged EU. In particular the enlargement process makes it necessary to reform the existing EU institutions and decision-making processes. Already 15 member states have adopted the constitution. The CDU/CSU Delegation, together with Chancellor Merkel, wants to reactivate the process of ratification in 2007.

By adopting the constitutional treaty, national and European competences at the policy level will be clarified, and national parliaments will be able to work more closely with the European institutions. Additional competences of the European Parliament will strengthen the legislative power and allow better democratic control and transparency. Furthermore, an instrument for a common foreign policy will be established. The constitution offers many answers to open questions which are subject to controversial public debate. Even if the German EU Presidency will not have enough time to solve the problem of the ratification of the constitutional treaty, it might be able to give an additional impetus to this process. Additional topics need to be included in further discussions, e.g. the European Energy Policy and social commitments.

The CDU/CSU Delegation accepts its responsibility of starting the discussion about the future of Europe in the European Parliament. The constitutional treaty will strengthen the European Union from the inside and will provide for a stronger Europe in the world.

The enlargement process of the European Union from 25 to 27 member states on January 1, 2007 is a big challenge, not only for the acceding states but also the bigger member countries. Until 2004 Spain, Great Britain, Italy, France and Germany were represented by two Commissioners each. Now, each country may nominate only one Member of the Commission. As a result, the Commission has lost a lot of its integrative power in the bigger member states. The European Parliament now has 732 members and will be elected in all 27 member states for the first time in summer 2009. As the member state with the largest population, Germany will keep its number of 99 Members of the European Parliament.

Another important question relating to the future of Europe concerns its borders. This is not only a geographical question. Many member states have different approaches to define the limits of enlargement. Some member states focus on deepening and strengthening the European Union with its 27 member states, others follow a strongly expansionist idea focused on economic and trade aspects of enlargement. Deepening integration on the one hand and economic extension on the other are challenging not only for the European institutions but also for the citizens of Europe. Therefore the CDU/CSU Delegation supports the idea that beyond 27 member states no new promises are being made to applicant countries. Even if some neighboring countries might oppose this decision, it is necessary to consolidate the European decision-making processes and the work of the European institutions. Otherwise the EU will risk loosing its competitiveness by giving up its workability. In the past, the Franco-German axis significantly influenced the development of the European Union as well as its enlargement. Christian Democratic Chancellors have dominated this relationship, such as Adenauer and Kohl, together with de Gaulle und Mitterrand, and the CDU/CSU delegation will support Chancellor Merkel to reactivate this axis again.

In general the criteria of Copenhagen are binding and need to be completely fulfilled by every applicant country. In addition the EU has to decide about other forms of partnership apart from full membership of the EU. Some proposals are already discussed, e.g. the 'special partnership' developed by the German CDU/CSU. Internal consolidation must have priority before further accession is possible. Europe has a great interest in economically strong, democratically developed and politically stable neighbouring countries; therefore forms of cooperation are needed. Stopping the accession process does not mean excluding countries which wish to have a close relationship with the EU. The CDU/CSU Delegation has no interest in asking too much of the EU by widening its cultural and geographic borders. As a consequence nationalism would harm the future integration process of the EU and weaken its global position. Therefore new ways of cooperation need to be adopted by the EU.

Europe also needs a common foreign and security policy as well as answers to the future of its energy supply and climate change. The EU has to strengthen the single market and expand the euro area, building a real alternative to the dollar and the yen. The member states cannot afford just to deal with national interests. In times of globalization European countries must use their possibility to be represented by the EU as an economic and political authority. The EU needs to clarify its aims and concepts for the next decades in order to convince the citizens of Europe without simply referring to the arguments of the past. The CDU/CSU Delegation in the European Parliaments recognizes the need to promote the common values of Europe, because the citizens must realize the value of the EU as an alternative to global pressure and insecure expectations in the future. When focusing on the global economic system, the Christian Democrats developed the 'new social market model' which transfers the economic achievements of the last 50 years in Europe and Germany to a global perspective. As a result, the CDU/CSU Delegation in European Parliament wants to align globalization with European values.

At present, expectations are high for the German EU Presidency in the first half of 2007. The German CDU/CSU Delegation will assist the German government with Chancellor Merkel in all aspects of its work.

Only a stable and strong European Union will be useful for our partners in the world when questions of globalizing markets and environmental challenges need to be solved in the future. Especially the good and successful cooperation with the growing Asian countries is from special interest, not only in within the framework of the WTO but also in bilateral conventions. Contacts between the European Union and equal partners from Asia and America will mainly influence the future world order.

Tradition, Identity and Future: Basic Issues Concerning a European Cultural Policy

Doris Pack

Member of the Committee on Culture and Education
Chairwoman of the Delegation for Relations
with the Countries of Southeast Europe
European Parliament

The focus on economic policy issues has for a very long time pushed culture, as the basis of the European idea, into the background of public consciousness. Yet a European identity does not evolve through the growth of the European market, but through the development and awareness of common values.

Europe is more than the combined gross national products of its member states. Indeed, despite many decades of political and military confrontation, Europe has never ceased to exist as a single cultural area. But our goal cannot be a Europe which seeks uniformity; instead, what we must aim for is a Europe united in its diversity, forging a common destiny, as the text of the Constitutional Treaty makes clear.

The European Union is ultimately the outcome of an historic learning process. The changed political situation and the return of the countries of Central and Eastern Europe have also refocused attention on the cultural dimension of the European integration project. There is a growing conviction that Europe's political, economic and social integration cannot be successful in the long term unless Europe grasps that it is a cultural community. The awareness of the cultural dimension must be heightened—this is the message now being sent out in speeches on Europe everywhere, notwithstanding all the differences between the European countries and nations, whose diversity is the real characteristic of their unity.

In his speech at the Frankfurt Book Fair in 1993, then President of the European Commission Jacques Delors commented on this state of affairs, saying that "without the engagement of intellectuals and people active in the cultural sphere... Europe cannot progress.... We need new ideas, for Europe must be given an entirely new face, and must be created intellectually." Culture has thus become a political issue for Europe: Europe's reunification with the countries of Central, Eastern and, soon, South-Eastern Europe has always been a common European task, taking place against the background of common values.

"Nothing is so powerful as an idea whose time has come," said Abraham Lincoln. European culture's time has come. It is therefore no coincidence that the Maastricht Treaty also contains a 'culture clause,' which provides a basis for action by the Community in the development of cultural policy initiatives and sets out the framework for this action. After decades in limbo due to the lack of any legal bases in the Treaty of Rome, this was a much-needed shift towards the establishment of cultural policy in Europe.

What is remarkable, from my perspective, is that expectations of the influence that culture can bring to bear have increased dramatically. Suddenly, attempts are now being made to burden cultural policy with the task that European economic policy has so far not fulfilled, namely to create a vibrant sense, among the European Union's citizens, that they belong together.

It would be unrealistic to hope or expect that efforts to assert European cultural unity could lead to the emergence of a European citizens' initiative in support of Europe's political union. It would exceed the bounds of a future European cultural policy to expect it to succeed where industrial, agricultural and economic policy has partly failed, namely to make European identity a living political reality.

What are the key features of European culture that distinguish it, for example, from American or African culture? What is its specifically European aspect?

First of all, Europe is not a melting pot like the United States. Each one of its constituent elements has its own history, its own culture and its own language—in short, its own identity.

European culture has a distinctive feature: it combines unity and diversity, individuality and openness in an often tense but entirely fruitful relationship. Plurality is thus both the characteristic and the hallmark of culture in Europe, whose other features are democracy and the rule of law, philosophy, religion and humanistic anthropology. The Charter of Fundamental Rights marks a breakthrough in value-based policy development and is a milestone in Europe's integration as a community of values. Never before has there been such a consensus in a globalized world, especially against the backdrop of a conflict-laden history—a history of brutal wars, enmity and religious schisms.

The strength of European culture lies in its differences: it is not what is 'typically European' that finds recognition and admiration throughout the world, but the diversity that Europe has produced in its national and regional cultures: in music, in art, in literature, and in its languages.

But the strength of European culture is also based on its capacity to integrate: for language and culture are very often not confined to a group or geographical area. That is why it is difficult to associate the term 'European culture' directly with a distinct geographical, historical, political, religious or cultural entity called 'Europe'.

Rather, Europe is a multicultural reality with some fifty more or less elite cultures in almost as many languages, dispersed across half a continent, whose borders are difficult to define and whose experiences of history are diverse and very rarely coincide with those of their neighbours.

We can thus conclude that there is not a distinct 'European' culture, but culture in Europe. Only culture which brings Europeans together and links Europe to the rest of the world deserves to be called 'European'.

Starting with this premise, it may be possible to develop a cultural policy perspective for Europe. But let us begin by defining what this type of policy should not, and must not, seek to achieve.

Such a policy should not aim to meld these cultures, these precious identities, these rich linguistic, historical and national distinctions, to create a European 'Frankenstein's monster'.

Nor should it aim to harmonize national and regional cultural distinctions. Rather, European cultural policy—as a policy undertaken within the framework of the European Union—should be guided strictly by the principle of subsidiarity and thus keep within the framework of European cultural federalism. Its task is therefore to promote the opportunities for all identities to express themselves, and to foster closer relations through mutual understanding and respect. In a world dominated by the market economy, Europe and its institutions should nurture and support the consistent development of European regional cultures; minority cultures must not be squeezed out or dominated in economic terms.

At the same time, however, the task is also to create and promote overarching structures which facilitate a European culture on a broader scale. That is why European cultural policy must, by its very nature, have an integrating effect. It must create frames of reference and enable European culture to have an impact on the wider world.

In radiating out to this wider world, European culture must convey something of the specific situation in which it developed, which can only be encountered in Europe. Or to quote Thomas Mann: Europe is "the opposite of provincial narrow-mindedness, boorish egoism, a nationalistic lack of sophistication, and ignorance."

The task of the European Union's cultural policy is thus to help ensure that Europe's culture, its trends and aspirations, can extend far beyond the Union's borders.

In specific terms, this means that the more quickly and comprehensively scientific and technical civilization links us and aligns our living conditions on a European and worldwide scale, the greater the need to safeguard the distinctive features of our national and regional origins, which enable European culture to be a culture of diversity and richness.

The more vigorously we maintain our specific cultures of origin in the European regions, the more visibly we must demonstrate the unity of European culture as well—the shared origins of our religious and moral culture, our legal culture, our literature and art, which enable us to identify ourselves and each other across all our national and regional borders.

The inclusion of the culture clause in the Maastricht Treaty finally enabled us to achieve much of what had previously featured on the 'wish list' for a European cultural policy. As a result, the Commission, as guardian of the Treaties, is now obliged to scrutinise the cultural compatibility of European measures.

This creates a global dimension, and therefore a wider significance, for cultural policy in the Union. This is especially important in preserving Europe's shared cultural heritage.

A further priority is fostering cooperation with third countries and the competent international organizations, in particular the Council of Europe, which has a far more comprehensive cultural policy tradition and experience than the EC/EU, and which was previously the only forum in which cultural work took place across national borders. The new cooperation here can therefore only be beneficial.

There is a general consensus between the member states, the Council, the Commission and the EP that the regions' diverse cultures must be integrated more fully into the EU's cultural policy activities; in this context, all the regions must be equal partners, regardless of their economic performance and status.

In line with this requirement, the EU does not maintain its own institutions or seek to replace the cultural promotion activities undertaken by the nations, regions, cities and private sponsors. In other words, it is not about grafting yet another institution with appropriate specialist departments onto the national ministries or regional bodies. The EU's approach is different: it does not replace existing cultural promotion, but complements it by contributing a European dimension. This takes place, for example, through the promotion of monuments with European significance, from the Acropolis to the monasteries of Mount Athos, the reconstruction of Lisbon's Old City, and the preservation of Baroque garden design. The annual designation of a European Capital of Culture also enhances the visibility of Europe's immense cultural diversity.

The EU also promotes Europe-wide cooperation between cultural institutions, artists and cultural events. It is also important to mention the grants available to young creative artists who choose to study or work in institutions outside their home country. Today, the Culture Programme is promoting mobility in Europe, but is also helping to develop and impart self-confidence and a sense of our European roots to a global, dynamically changing world. The task of bringing together the diverse national cultures in European unity must be planned, organised, experienced and practised at all levels—at city, regional, national and European level. The European Union can thus serve as an example for other regions of the world—the ASEAN countries, the League of Arab States, the African Union and NAFTA, all of which are developing their own supranational structures and, in doing so, are guided by the only functioning model currently in existence, namely the European Union.

The EU's approach is to support all facets of creative endeavour—exchange, cooperation, broadening experience, and promoting intercultural dialogue in Europe. What this means in practice, in every case, is dialogue between people.

Europe's great opportunity in the coming years lies not in its sociocultural unity and homogeneity but in facilitating cultural diversity. This means that a European cultural policy, if it is to be successful, must find a pragmatic response to the cultural developments taking place in the modern industrial society and to the cultural policy challenges posed by the European integration process.

Above all, the cultural role of the audiovisual sector has a huge impact; we must be careful to ensure that pure competition and audience figures do not become the dominant factors here. Far more money flows into this sector than into the traditional fields of art mentioned above. The EU's MEDIA Programme, for example, promotes training for professionals in the European audiovisual industry. It also supports the development of European production projects and works in this sector.

The UNESCO Convention on the Protection and Promotion of the Diversity of Cultural Expressions has been approved by the EU as a whole. This opens up a new international field of activity in which European cultural policy can prove its worth.

However, the real challenge facing cultural policy at European level must be the intellectual and emotional safeguarding of plurality, tolerance, freedom and democracy. This is the core area of political, historical and cultural development whose importance cannot be overstated.

We all have a vision of a better and more peaceful world. Culture can contribute in many different ways to giving this vision form and content—in other words, to its artistic expression.

A European cultural policy must vigorously promote networks to breathe life into the abstract consensus of our community of values and integrate it into daily life, encourage a real sense of community and foster dialogue. There is a clear role here for the institutions of the EU, the Member States, the regions, the cities and civil society.

Finally, a message for all those who are critical of culture: it is true that culture can be challenging, for it has sharp edges and corners. Culture deals with the past, records the present and gives voice to longings and nostalgia. This is not always comfortable, and may provoke criticism among those affected by it. Certainly, without culture, life might well be easier, more comfortable and less problematical—but it would also be infinitely poorer!

The United States and Its Relations with the European Union

Elmar Brok, MEP

Chairman of the Committee of Foreign Affairs (1999–2007)

In recent years, commercial relations between the United States of America and the European Union have reached a stage of deep integration. However, so far both the policy making as well as the legislative and regulatory systems in Europe and the U.S. have failed to incorporate a strong transatlantic dimension. In order to further strengthen the transatlantic ties and to set the relationship between the United States and the European Union on a solid basis, an overarching framework of co-operation is needed.

Today, regulatory differences constitute the most significant barriers to transatlantic trade relations. Regulations are often developed in complete isolation from one another and consequently run the risk of posing significant difficulties for economic actors on both sides of the Atlantic. The most prominent examples for such regulatory initiatives are would improve regulation and minimise regulatory disagreements. It would also help to advance transatlantic trade and commerce.

The European Parliament and the U.S. Congress have already put in place the Transatlantic Legislators' Dialogue (TLD) in order to better coordinate policy initiatives as well as regulatory and legislative proposals of mutual interest. Moreover, the Transatlantic Economic Partnership and the Transatlantic Business Dialogue have been established to form a platform for exchange in matters regarding commerce, justice, transport and treasury/finance. However, without the absence of binding commitments, difficulties remain. The European Parliament has therefore called for the adoption of a Transatlantic Partnership Agreement by 2007 to strengthen the EU-U.S. relationship. The European Parliament has also stressed the need to reinforce the parliamentary dimension of the transatlantic partnership by transforming the TLD into a Transatlantic Assembly. At a later stage the establishment of a Transatlantic Market is also envisaged. This vision has recently been endorsed by the U.S. Senate, which adopted a resolution in December 2006, urging the United States and the European Union to work together to strengthen the Transatlantic Market that shall be completed by 2015.

So far coordination is mainly based on voluntary efforts made by various regulatory agencies. It is crucial that those are complemented by an overarching agreement between the United States and the European Union. This agreement should be drawn up in co-operation between the U.S. Congress and the White House on one side and the EU institutions, the European Parliament, the Council and Commission, on the other. The agreement should oblige legislative and regulatory authorities to consider the potential impact of their acts on transatlantic economic relations. It should also lay out simple but effective means of communication to avoid conflicting or burdensome legislation whenever possible. The groundwork for concluding such an agreement in 2008 should already start during the next U.S.-EU Summit in 2007. The U.S. Congress and the European Parliament need to be involved in this process that is due to set out the priorities for implementing the agreement.

The transatlantic trade and investment ties have never been stronger. Therefore, we need an institutionalized dialogue to create a barrier-free transatlantic market and a system to settle bilateral trade disputes. Such an institutionalized cooperation would neither affect the sovereignty of the U.S. nor the EU. On the contrary, a further economic integration of our markets would reinforce our economic strengths and international competitiveness for the years to come. Only a joint approach would enable the transatlantic community to establish an economic stronghold and to strengthen their respective and common business sectors in a non-defensive manner against emerging economic powers such as India, China, Russia and Brazil.

However, we have to strengthen transatlantic ties, not just because of economic reasons but especially because of political ones. We both share common values and interests. We wish to provide our citizens with peace, prosperity and security. We want to combat global terrorism, prevent the spread of weapons of mass destruction, enhance economic development and global stability, advance the Middle East peace process and prevent violent conflicts. However, securing those values has become increasingly complex and depends on decisions taken in different regions of the world.

The last decade has proven how quickly but nevertheless sustainable our volatile environment can influence the parameters of foreign politics. The process of globalization is leading to an increasingly interconnected economy. The threat of terrorism, the fall of the Iron Curtain and the rise of new economic powers such as India and China are just a few examples. It is difficult to foresee the challenges ahead and to anticipate the geographical dimension of threats. Nation states may try as hard as they can to protect their interests but neither of us can meet these challenges alone. We cannot help but stand together with others who share our values. In the light of today's global power relations a self-contained realization of national interests has become unrealistic—in Europe as well as in the United States.

In Europe, for a long time, there was no such thing as a Common Foreign and Security Policy (CFSP). It remained the dream of a few visionaries to establish a European counterbalance against the two super powers, Russia and the United States. The EU's CFSP was finally established as the second pillar of the European Union in 1993 with the Maastricht Treaty. Since then, a number of important changes have been introduced, e.g. by the European Councils of Amsterdam, Laeken and Nice. Within a little more than a decade, the CFSP has evolved considerably and at amazing speed. Interim structures have now become powerful permanent instruments.

Some of the EU's endeavors in foreign and security policy have become success stories. European diplomacy is gaining increasing influence. For instance, in the Former Yugoslav Republic of Macedonia (FYROM), the High Representative was able to prevent a civil war. Similarly, in the Ukraine, Javier Solana, the European Parliament and Polish President Kwasniewski provided successful mediation. However, with the increasing scope assumed by the CFSP, responsibilities as well as expectations have grown. The EU's ability to achieve the diplomatic success to which it aspires has been questioned. Other shortcomings and inefficiencies of EU foreign policy were revealed in the past, notably the diplomatic and military failures in the Balkans or the quarrels with the U.S. over the approach to the Iraq crisis, which in the end even led to division among the EU partners.

The central question therefore is: What are the perspectives and limits for the EU's CFSP in the future? Especially in the realm of foreign and security policy, the quick growth of European cooperation in recent years has made swift reform of its institutional structure necessary. We need the Constitution for Europe to prepare the EU for the challenges of the new century through the introduction of new, more efficient mans in CFSP. Some of the key developments will be outlined below.

Towards a European Culture of Security

A topic which is increasingly incorporated in agreements between the EU and its international partners is security. Consequently, it becomes ever more important for the Union to clarify what shape its security policy should take. The member states need to adopt a common understanding on this matter: a European Culture of Security.

In the 21st century, it has become evident that security cannot be provided by military means alone, nor can it be based on just one country's national powers. This is the credo the EU laid down in its Security Strategy of December 2003. New threats, such as terrorism, the proliferation of weapons of mass destruction, failed states and the concomitant privatization of force, regional conflicts in the Middle East, South Asia and the Korean peninsula and organized crime demand an integrated approach to security policies. This must comprise military instruments and capabilities alike, ranging from conflict prevention to "nation building."

The European Security Strategy, which was fully supported by the European Parliament, pursues three strategic goals: coping with various threats; creating security in the EU Neighborhood; and supporting an international order based on an effective multilateralism. It specifies the EU's ambition to be a credible actor in security matters. The strategy calls on the Union to become more active, more capable, and more coherent in pursuing its security objectives through increased capabilities, the pooling of assets, stronger diplomatic capacity, and common threat assessments. The strategy puts an emphasis on partnership with the United States and NATO, calling the transatlantic relationship "irreplaceable" and noting the central role of the Berlin Plus arrangements in crisis management.

The Union seeks to handle crises more actively and above all to prevent them. It will develop the necessary diplomatic, military and industrial capabilities with greater determination and will make more coherent use of its different instruments of foreign policy. An example for the EU's intention to implement this comprehensive approach is the military mission "ALTHEA" in Bosnia-Herzegovina, which adds in a significant way to the EU's political engagement, its assistance programmes and its ongoing police and monitoring missions. The European approach particularly focuses on combining civil and military elements of crisis management. The crisis in Kosovo made us realize that only a regional approach can really ensure peace, providing it addresses aspects of security, of democratic, constitutional and legal principles, of human rights and last but not least economic development, not all at once but all at the same time and with the same weight.

Yet the possibility for the EU to guarantee security remained the missing link for a long time. Only the progress achieved in the past five years is bringing the EU closer to closing that gap and to hold in one hand the above- mentioned diplomatic, economic and military instruments and capabilities, with which it can emerge as a credible actor in international crisis management. European security policy is still in its infancy and shows signs of fragmentation. The common Security Strategy set the framework. The outlines are already visible and the competence areas are gradually becoming clearer: 7,000 EURFOR soldiers in Bosnia-Herzegovina, plus police, reconstruction programs (CARDs) and stability and association agreements (SAP). The EU acts at once as a protecting power, as a reconstruction partner and as a provider of a general perspective for the country.

With European diplomacy being increasingly successful, the perspective will remain a global one rather than being limited to the European context. Many conflicts will only be resolved together with our American partners. The Middle East, for instance, belongs to that category. The EU will not be able to avoid certain responsibilities much longer where the UN asks it, where it receives a mandate and where its presence is requested by both sides of the conflict. This development might soon also be illustrated by an EU-mission in the Democratic Republic of Congo, where EU forces might be providing security for the presidential and parliamentary elections. These same responsibilities would apply if a mission was coordinated with the U.S.

and thus with NATO, and if such crisis management was to be accepted by the European public. This is where the European Parliament together with National Parliaments must initiate an opinion-forming debate.

The European Security Strategy has delivered an analysis of the threats and a definition of European security interests. Now further institutional elements for forming a modern EU defense policy are being developed. The EU Member States agreed to the concept of battle groups, the headline goal for the forces in 2010 and the creation of a European Defense Agency. It is this mosaic of individual decisions in the framework of the Security Strategy that lays the foundation for the growth of a genuine European security culture.

A Strong Partnership as Foundation for a Strong Foreign Policy

Last but not least, it must be emphasized that the increasing cooperation between European countries is only one step towards an effective foreign and security policy. If Europe really wants to be heard in the world it needs to find strong partners who share its values and interests. In the United States the EU has an important and reliable international partner. Our history shows many good examples for how we can best join forces to achieve our common goals. It is now time to reinforce the transatlantic partnership in order to respond to, lead and shape the new global realities. It is this kind of solid cooperation between our regions that we need in order to master the challenges of foreign and security policy lying ahead of us. We need to share responsibilities for the sake of our common interests.

Towards a European Security and Defense Union

Karl von Wogau, MEP

Chairman of the Subcommittee on Security and Defence

One of the main ideas behind the economic integration in Europe after the Second World War was to ensure peace and stability in Europe. But although European unity was from the very beginning a project to safeguard peace, common security and defence policy came about relatively late. After the Second World War European economic integration made rapid progress while political integration remained weak. At the end of the Cold War the European Union was an economic giant but a dwarf as far as foreign and security policy was concerned.

In 1989, the American philosopher Francis Fukuyama announced the "End of History." But by 1991, when Yugoslavia collapsed in chaos and violence, it became clear that this would not come about.

It was to Europe's shame that we were unable to take the necessary action to prevent or at least mitigate civil war in the Balkans. Eight thousand people lost their lives in Srebrenica alone, while the powerful economies of the European Union stood on the sidelines, unable to take decisive preventive action.

The Balkans are part of the immediate neighborhood of the European Union, but Europe's individual member states failed by proving incapable of pooling their efforts and stopping the massacres. At the time, the European Union as such had neither the means nor the instruments of joint intervention by armed forces. We needed the help of our American allies to end this civil war on the Balkans.

During this period many Europeans felt that we had to do everything in our power to prevent a situation like this from ever happening again. The starter's gun for a European Security and Defense Policy went off as it became apparent at the British-French 1998 summit in Saint Malo that not only France, but also Great Britain was committing itself actively to the project of a European defense component. Since that time, European Security and Defense Policy (ESDP) has developed rapidly. At the 1999 summit in Cologne EU heads of state and governments decided to set up a crisis intervention force numbering 60,000 soldiers. One year later, they resolved to build up a police force comprising 5,000 men. The first mission of soldiers under European command took place in the Former Yugoslav Republic of Macedonia in 2003 where the EU took over the security tasks from NATO. The military operation "Artemis" in Congo was also conducted in 2003 to stabilize an explosive situation in the district of Ituri.

Since then, the European Union has assumed responsibility for peace and stability in various parts of the world by numerous military and civilian missions and operations. At present, 6,200 soldiers are deployed under European command in Bosnia-Herzegovina, where the European Union has taken the responsibility for securing peace. At the same time, multiple police and rule of law missions are going on in many parts of the world. The European Security and Defense Policy has been the most dynamic policy area of the European Union in the last few years.

Since the end of the Cold War, the threats confronting Europe have fundamentally changed. The Soviet Union and the Warsaw Pact have disappeared. But international terrorism, the proliferation of weapons of mass destruction and regional conflicts at the borders of the European Union are the threats to the citizens of Europe today. Opinion polls demonstrate that a large majority of the citizens of the European Union is aware of these threats and therefore favors a common foreign and security policy of the member states.

The citizens want less Europe when it comes to detailed regulations of everyday life and more Europe in the fight against organized crime and terrorism. Intensified European collaboration in the field of security and defense policy is thus not only of key importance for the security of the people in Europe, but also for the acceptance of the European Union.

On November 16, 2006, the European Parliament adopted by a large majority (414 for, 117 against, with 12 abstentions) a resolution on the implementation of the European Security Strategy (A6-0366/2006) that I prepared as Chairman of the European Parliament's Subcommittee on Security and Defense. This resolution calls for the further development of the European Union into a "European Security and Defense Union" and contains a number of proposals aiming at improving the common ability to act in the fields of foreign policy, security and defense.

Decisionmaking Structures

We have to ensure more transparent decision making processes in the field of ESDP and adequate parliamentary scrutiny by the Parliaments of the Member States and the European Parliament. It is important that decision making in foreign affairs happens in a way comprehensible for the citizens. They should know who bears the responsibility for which decision. Unfortunately this is not really the case so far.

European foreign and security policy needs a face. Javier Solana, High Representative for the Common Foreign and Security Policy (CFSP) and Secretary-General of the Council of the European Union, is presently performing this task very successfully despite the fact that he has insufficient means at his disposal. The High Representative does not dispose of an adequate administration of foreign affairs. Moreover, he has to share his responsibilities with the European Commission.

Therefore, in order to improve the decision making structures at the European level, the Parliament calls for a European Minister of Foreign Affairs who is at the same time Vice-President of the Commission as foreseen in the Constitutional Treaty, a European Deputy Foreign Minister in charge of security and defense policy, and a European civil protection force as proposed in the report of the former French Minister of Foreign Affairs Michel Barnier.

Civil and Military Capabilities

The European Parliament calls also for an improvement of the European Union's set of civil and military capabilities. To improve European disaster response, the Parliament stresses the need to fill the gaps in the area of strategic transport and highlights the gaps in terms of telecommunications and intelligence. It is often said that European defense budgets are too small and should be increased, and that duplications between the European Union and NATO have to be avoided. This is certainly true. However we must point to the fact that duplications between the member states of the European Union are even more damaging when we endeavor to improve the European capabilities.

While the European Union's member states individually spend a total sum of more than 170 billion euros per year on defense, their ability to act is often limited by the absence of key capabilities. After the Kosovo war we were told by our American allies that we were spending almost half of their effort on defense but that the efficiency of our contribution was only ten percent.

This relative European inefficiency is partly due to the fact that we do not have a common European defense equipment market. This leads to much unnecessary duplication of procurement programs. At present, we have five national telecommunications systems for running multinational operations. Soldiers criticize that some of these different telecommunication systems are not even compatible with each other. The troops employed under European command need a joint telecommunication system. A common system would be less costly, more efficient and less risky for the personnel running these operations.

At this time, technical innovation is taking place in this field: Software defined radio. We should not miss this opportunity to develop a common European basic standard which would be used by the armed forces, police and desaster management organizations. This would also correspond to the broad definition of security in the European Security Strategy.

In Finland, for instance, this is the case today already. Armed forces, police and disaster control services of this country can encrypt their telecommunications independently of each other, but in case of need they are able to communicate with each other within the scope of the same system.

Satellite reconnaissance in Europe is another classic example for inefficiency by unnecessary duplications. We need satellite reconnaissance for joint European missions and for supervising our common European external borders. Information, which we jointly need, should also be jointly collected. But this is so far not the case. The results of the national satellite reconnaissance systems “Helios”, “SAR

Lupe" (a high resolution radar satellite system) and "Cosmo Skymed" are not available to all member states. A joint European system would be more cost-effective and better here. A particularly serious grievance is the fact that the Battle Groups of the European Union, which are now about to be organized, do not have uniform and full access to aerial and satellite-based reconnaissance.

The protection of the common European external borders—a key challenge for the protection of the citizens in Europe—also requires better and compatible equipment of the border police forces and a joint European approach for an integrated management in the surveillance of the borders.

For all types of missions it is imperative that command structure, equipment and armament of European troops are both adequate and efficient. Soldiers are exposed to unnecessary dangers if the command structure or the equipment and armament do not meet the requirements. The use of different and often incompatible equipment in multinational operations lowers efficiency and raises cost and risks.

We also have to consider that multinational operations like Congo and Lebanon become more costly by the fact that due to the different equipment parallel chains of supply have to be organized. It would therefore be a big step forward if the equipment of the battle groups which are being established now would gradually be harmonized. This could begin with the systems of reconnaissance and telecommunications. Efforts should therefore be made to provide the units operating under the command of the Union with modern and compatible and, at best, standardized equipment.

In view of the generally scarce public budgets in the EU the necessary improvement of the technical capacities can only be achieved if the available budgetary means are used more efficiently. This could be managed by avoiding unnecessary duplications and parallel developments and by creating a joint European market for armaments.

European Security Strategy

In spite of the rapid development since 1999, the armed forces available to the European Union for quick intervention outside of its territory are limited in number. It is thus of decisive importance that the European Union does not scatter its numerically limited forcers without any plan over the globe, but pursues a clear strategy which builds on common European interests. The safeguarding of peace and stability in our neighborhood is a central European security interest. The European Union should therefore concentrate its newly developed capacities in the security field primarily to our geographical neighborhood.

The security strategy of the European Union contains an excellent analysis of the perils of the modern world, but no concrete detailed formulation of the European interests yet and no concepts for transforming the strategy into concrete measures. The European Parliament calls for a regular updating of the European Security Strategy. Both the Parliaments of the Member States and the European Parliament should be involved in the preparation of this strategy. This would also allow a broad public debate about the goals and approaches of the ESDP. A regular updating of the strategy could also help to develop a strategy dialogue between Europe and the United States, which submits a new version of its national security strategy in each legislative period.

Risks and Responses

The security risks that the European Union faces today are of multiple natures and require different responses. In case of an attack by armed forces of a third country against the territory of the European Union, NATO will, for the majority of the member countries of the European Union, continue to be the best suited instrument and guarantor of our common security.

Apart from the scenario of an attack by armed forces there are, however, other security risks and challenges with which the European Union has to deal. If it is, for example, about destroying the financial networks of organized crime or international terrorism, enhancing police cooperation, securing the common European external borders, protecting critical infrastructures or coordinating the controls at the airports, it is the European Union which has the appropriate means and possibilities and which is therefore required to act.

Homeland security is an essential element of the security policy of the United States. Compared to that, this task is being mentioned only in passing in the European Security Strategy of 2003. At the European level we should continuously work on the development and implementation of joint European concepts for homeland security. The planned attacks on airliners to the United States prevented in Great Britain in August 2006 have again demonstrated the necessity of comprehensive and internationally coordinated security concepts.

In safeguarding peace and stability in our geographic neighbourhood, the European Union bets rightly on a close interlinking between civilian and military crisis management. The experiences of the past years clearly show that a successful and lasting management of crises and conflicts can only succeed if the different measures—be it military or civilian ones—are closely interacting.

The most important feature of the ESDP is the close coordination between most different instruments. With regard to its limited capacities Europe must carefully consider in this context which of the tasks it will take on. But as soon as Europe decides to support the solution of a conflict or to cope with a problem it must incorporate these efforts into an overall concept, which also takes account of other problems, risks and dangers associated with that.

Thus, the military operation of the European Union to provide security for the 2006 election in the Democratic Republic of Congo will make sense in the long term only if it will be included in an overall concept for the build-up of a constitutionally and economically viable Congo. There is always the risk that the view of correlations and circumstances is obscured by ad-hoc mandates, which are limited in respect to area, time and subject. Problems are sometimes tackled as if they were hovering in a vacuum.

Meanwhile, the European Union has gathered considerable experience in interlinking peacemaking and peacekeeping measures, crisis management, the build-up of democratic structures, the setup of functioning administrations, cooperation in development projects and crime prevention. The coordination between civilian and military instruments must be further extended as a central trademark of the ESDP.

In addition to the protection of its own territory and the safeguarding of peace and stability in our geographic neighborhood the European Union must be capable of conducting humanitarian missions under the mandate of the United Nations and evacuating citizens of the European Union from crisis areas all over the world. In the future, the evacuation of Europeans from crisis regions ought to be organized in a better way than this was the case in July 2006 in Lebanon. It is contradictory to the basic idea of mutual solidarity if each member state of the European Union, which possesses the necessary means, starts to evacuate its own citizens while the citizens of smaller European countries must just hope to be given a lift. The evacuation of Europeans from smaller member states must not depend on the fact whether or not a larger member state has still spaces available on its ship or airplane. Moreover, all should be evacuated in the most secure way and not in the way, which the respective country can afford. The evacuation of Europeans from crisis regions is a matter which requires European solidarity. Here, the European Union should have combined capacities for joint evacuation and rescue missions.

Still a Lot to Do

It is widely recognized within governments and society in Europe that the risks and challenges of the post-Cold War international security environment require regional and multilateral cooperation in the field of security and defense. That goes for Europe and for other regions of the world, too.

In a world in which no state or region can meet security challenges alone, Europe will continue to strengthen its common Security and Defense Policy. At the same time Europe will remain steadfast in its commitment to upholding and developing international law. The European Security Strategy states:

"In a world of global threats, global markets and global media, our security and prosperity increasingly depend on an effective multilateral system. The development of a stronger international society, well functioning international institutions and a rule-based international order is our objective."

The European Union will continue to strengthen its cooperation with other world regions in order to reinforce shared values and promote common interests towards an effective multilateral world order.

International Cooperation in the Konrad Adenauer Foundation

Gerhard Wahlers

Director, International Division, Konrad Adenauer Foundation, Berlin

In their overall range, approximately one half of the tasks set down by the Konrad Adenauer Foundation (KAF) pertain to Germany and the other half to projects of international cooperation worldwide. At present, the Foundation is represented abroad by 84 staff members in more or less as many overseas branches and foreign offices in the most important centers of political decision-making worldwide. They are assisted in their work in the Foundation's countries of activity by-on the whole-well over 300 local employees, and their programs implemented for the most part in cooperation with just as many partner organizations. The planning, coordination and steering of these international tasks is undertaken in the main division "International Cooperation" (INT), which is presently run with 73 staff members in Berlin.

For over 40 years, the Konrad Adenauer Foundation has been making a distinct contribution to development policy in the Third World as part of its efforts to promote democracy and establish the rule of law worldwide. From the very outset, the Foundation was intent on extending help for self-help while cooperating in a spirit of partnership within the framework of the projects supported. It is for this reason that by far the largest proportion of the funds at our disposal is invested in development activities. It is our endeavor to gain acceptance worldwide for the liberal-constitutional model of democracy based on the rule of law, even under the difficult conditions created by globalization. In doing so, we also seek to underline the positive sides of globalization, while helping the developing and newly industrializing countries grasp the opportunities offered them by this process. Other focal areas of our activity in these countries are: furthering democratic-liberal development through education and consultancy; promoting the small and medium sector and establishing a regulatory policy; political decentralization; strengthening the role of women in society; rural development; academic and scientific cooperation; strengthening parties from the political center and promoting measures for environmental protection.

This apart, the Konrad Adenauer Foundation is also represented in the capitals of several European countries as well as in Washington. Here we are primarily concerned with strengthening and further advancing the process of European unification, particularly in the transition countries of Eastern and South Eastern Europe, and with furthering transatlantic relations. The collapse of the Soviet empire and of the communist dictatorships brought in its wake lasting changes in the political reality of Europe—changes that were positive in nature. Since reunification, Germany has not only acquired greater standing in international politics but also assumed fresh responsibilities in many areas. Europe has grown freer and more open. Meanwhile, eight countries from Central and Eastern Europe, which until just a few years ago had been shut off by the Iron Curtain from political and economic developments in Western Europe, have now been admitted into the European Union. The Konrad Adenauer Foundation has helped these countries overcome the hurdles en route to EU membership through political consultancy and education work. Likewise, the Foundation is also providing guidance to the countries of South Eastern Europe in the process of transition underway there, so that the unification of Europe is achieved in the manner envisaged by our founding fathers.

From the outset, the furtherance of democracy and the rule of law has been particularly central to our work. Included therein is also consultancy relating to constitutional issues which we provided with great success in Mongolia and Afghanistan, for instance. Only in democratic orders can human and civil rights be fully implemented; only between democratic states can lasting peace be secured and the peaceful resolution of conflicts set down as an obligation. Other subjects related to this area of activity are the social market economy, the entire sphere of the media and the improvement of the political, social and ecological basis of existence of vast numbers of people. The Foundation's range of activities is further supplemented by innumerable programs for dialogue on foreign and economic policy as well as on value-related or religious issues. Furthermore, thanks to our international networks, close contacts are maintained worldwide with democratic political parties from the center, and political developments in the countries where the Foundation is engaged observed and analyzed.

Thus, in thematically summing up the range of areas covered by the goals and tasks before us, it may be said that the international activities of the Konrad Adenauer Foundation encompass the following issues:

- deepening and extending European integration by promoting the debate on Europe in the EU Member States and by supporting the newly acceded countries;
- strengthening the transatlantic community of values while paying special attention to security relations and the German-American-Jewish dialogue;
- supporting the growth of democratic political framework conditions in Latin America, Africa, the Middle East as well as Asia as a prerequisite for improving the economic, social and ecological basis of existence;
- cooperating with political groups and parties from the center;
- linking up competition and social responsibility worldwide (commitment to the social market economy, and that too on a global basis);
- involvement in active crisis prevention and conflict management;
- support to internationally active NGO networks and multilateral organizations;
- building up a broad national consensus for tackling the effects of globalization.

For the Foundation to successfully tackle these pivotal tasks, an increasing measure of networking is necessary between international experts. In this connection, the country offices and overseas branches of the Foundation serve as important service and information centers while also providing a public forum for German interests in the host country concerned. Our offices in Washington and Brussels serve as hubs of this international presence. They ensure that the issues that are central to our work, such as the transatlantic partnership, European integration and, increasingly also, questions of international security, remain to the fore.

To realize our objectives we start out by engaging at various levels—collaborating with government agencies (local, regional and national), with academic institutions and organizations from civil society. Our relationship with our partner organizations is marked by a lasting sense of trust, and by an awareness of our common values—values that get manifested in the process of seeking out political solutions in a spirit of partnership. Together, all these contacts guarantee access to influential personalities and intellectual resources; they enable us expand our contacts to parties and international organizations of similar outlook and convictions and facilitate a global transfer of knowledge.

Activities that form the two main pillars of the Konrad Adenauer Foundation's international work, namely furtherance of democracy and consultancy relating to the rule of law, are steered and coordinated in regional programs. That is why we are constantly working to upgrade and expand our regional programs for the advancement of the rule of law and promotion of the media. In this context, the following programs are particularly noteworthy:

1. *Programs for the Promotion of the Rule of Law in South America, Central America and the Caribbean*, whose overriding objective is to support the process of democratization in these regions and contribute to the development and consolidation of an efficient legal system that is in accordance with the principles of the rule of law. At present, there is a special requirement for education and advisory services in the area of constitutional law, protection of human rights and measures for fighting corruption.

2. *Regional Programs for the Promotion of Democracy and the Media in Latin America and Sub-Saharan Africa*. Within the ambit of these programs, the Konrad Adenauer Foundation has been supporting the further development of the media landscape and the improvement in journalistic standards in Latin America and Africa since the eighties. In cooperation with local and regional partners, the KAF's media programs initiate and support the international and regional exchange of news, opin-

ions and ideas in the area of journalism. We promote cooperation within and between democratically minded media institutions, support the training of journalists and foster a sense of responsibility for balanced and competent reporting.

3. *The Regional Program for South East Asia: Politics and Media* based in Singapore promotes the transfer of knowledge between European think tanks and consultancy institutions and the region of South East Asia through regular meets. That apart, the regional office provides the East and Southeast Asia Network for Better Local Governments a platform to further develop its programs in the area of decentralization.

At present, similar programs are being conceived for other regions, as well as with the aim of developing a network for a global regulatory policy. In doing so, new measures shall be developed and regulated in the two areas of development cooperation and democracy as well as in response to the impacts of globalization and the opportunities it offers. The aim here is to promote in governmental and non-governmental actors a common understanding of the various aspects of the on-going process of globalization, both in the developing and newly industrializing countries as well as in the economically advanced democracies. Further, it is our aim to provide a platform for dialogue and for evolving common positions between these actors in the areas of society and state, economy and social order as well as on ethical issues—positions that will serve as elements of a global regulatory policy. In doing so we seek to extend support on the basis of both the value-determined criteria set down in German development cooperation as well as on the basis of the positions for a global regulatory policy evolved together with our partners in the developing countries. With differences in starting conditions being duly considered, these positions shall help formulate strategies for steering the processes of globalization both at the national and regional levels, and for tackling their effects in the developing countries. This is the only way to systematically gear up to the opportunities that the on-going processes of globalization offer while pursuing the main goals of German development cooperation (namely poverty alleviation, protection of human rights, development of civil society, enhanced political participation).

The dialogue between cultures and religions constitutes one of the major assets of international cooperation. Since the beginning of the sixties, the exchange between Christians and Jews has formed one of our core areas of activity. Today it is complemented by programs for dialogue between Christians and Muslims, which fall within the ambit of the comprehensive special program "Dialogue with Islam." This "Dialogue with Islam" likewise transcends national boundaries and is closely oriented to issues of political relevance that are significant today both in Germany as well as in the Islamic world. However the subject of this dialogue is generally not religious in nature but involves the effects of globalization, democratic models as solutions and a shared responsibility for the world.

With its dialogue programs in particular, the Konrad Adenauer Foundation makes a distinct contribution towards promoting a thinking oriented to the rule of law, towards peaceful conflict resolution and the fostering of Christian Democratic principles worldwide. At the same time, in many countries, we are also capable of assisting in the processes of market economy consolidation, democratic participation and political conflict management. In this way we help represent German interests at the international level and participate in the process of creating an international order that facilitates the establishment of peace and justice.

In the light of changes effected in the global framework conditions, it becomes clear that security, foreign, economic and development policy are increasingly being fused into one whole. Questions relating to development policy are increasingly being posed in security policy too. Imparting basic ethical values as part of the effort to promote democracy in international cooperation is development policy and security policy rolled into one. By drawing upon its global network of partner organizations, which participate at strategic points in the processes of policy-shaping, the Konrad Adenauer Foundation can address these challenges flexibly and adequately.

The Foundation brings out monographs and anthologies on socially relevant themes worldwide. In our monthly bulletin *KAS-Auslandsinformationen* (*KAF Foreign News*), the expertise of our overseas staff is made available to an expert readership in Germany. The executive summary is published in English.

Through its scheme of scholarships and course-supplementing programs, the Konrad Adenauer Foundation supports not only students living in Germany but also talented students and graduates from abroad. Selected candidates are assisted by the Foundation both materially and non-materially during their stay in Germany. Apart from building up their specialized skills, these students are helped—through the course-supplementing program—to develop their capacity to tackle tasks, both in public life and in society, with a sense of responsibility. That is why, while selecting candidates, social commitment and personal qualities are just as important as performance in the area of specialization. As of today, a total of 7700 German and 2000 foreign students have completed their study program with the assistance of the Konrad Adenauer Foundation.

At present, the Foundation's main division "International Cooperation" faces challenges that are indeed tremendous. The situation on the international security front (terrorism), the threat of disintegration of states (Afghanistan, Iraq, Liberia, among others) and the effects of globalization felt worldwide call for fresh responses. At the same time we are also confronted by the problem of a growing scarcity of funds. To effectively address these challenges we must concentrate more than ever before on our core tasks—of promoting democracy, extending advisory services for the establishment and consolidation of the rule of law, developing the media and the social market economy –while pooling all the resources at our disposal. However, even where conditions prove adverse, we will remain true to our commitment to help establish basic democratic values, stabilize politically and socially just regulatory models and contribute to the peaceful resolution of conflicts.

Fostering Transatlantic Dialogue: Aims and Objectives of the Konrad Adenauer Foundation Washington

Norbert Wagner

Director Konrad Adenauer Foundation Washington

The change in government in Germany in autumn 2005 ushered in a new chapter in transatlantic and German-American relations. After years of more or less open discord and conflict as well as a partial breakdown in the lines of communication between the two governments, the assumption of office by Chancellor Angela Merkel marks a new beginning.

On both sides of the Atlantic, this new beginning is based on the belief that joint action is a necessity, given the increasing number of common challenges facing Europe and America. Equally important in this regard is both the newfound awareness and recollection of shared values. President George W. Bush's visit to Brussels in spring 2005 itself was a clear indication of the high priority he accorded American-European relations. His visit to the EU institutions also demonstrated that due to growing international challenges, the U.S. is increasingly becoming dependent on the support of reliable partners. At a time when doubts were often raised in Europe regarding American interest in ensuring the success of the project of the European Union, there was a growing realization in the U.S. that it would be easier to resolve the multitude of problems besetting the world jointly rather than alone—in fact that problems could only, perhaps, best be resolved jointly.

Thus, the new beginning to European-American and German-American relations has also consistently been welcomed and supported in Washington. At times the euphoria in Washington was somewhat alarming because of the marks left by years of strained relations, which would not be so easy to forget. Consequently there is now a danger that expectations might be so high that it would be difficult to realize them fully, even with the best of intentions.

The Konrad Adenauer Foundation in Washington seeks to foster and intensify this new beginning in German-American and European-American relations by generating a dialogue through a broad network of multipliers on both sides of the Atlantic, by organizing a series of lectures and seminars, discussions among experts, specialist conferences, workshops and visits by delegations as well as by disseminating information.

Foreign and Security Policy: Common Challenges

In this context, foreign and security policy issues have long been the foremost priority within the dialogue program of the Konrad Adenauer Foundation (KAS) in Washington. The war in Iraq, the stabilization of Afghanistan, the global war against terror, the risk of nuclear proliferation (e.g. in Iran and North Korea), the fostering of stability and democracy in the Middle East and in Africa, relations with Russia and China are all issues that the Konrad Adenauer Foundation in Washington is continuously pursuing as part of its dialogue program. These are challenges that neither party could normally resolve alone. Of course, even in the future, there will continue to be areas, where it will be difficult, if not altogether impossible, to find commonalities or to avoid conflict. However, on both sides of the Atlantic, the golden rule would be to resolve these differences in an atmosphere of confidence and trust and of partnership. One of the most important tasks of the Konrad Adenauer Foundation in Washington is to create precisely this atmosphere of trust and confidence or to resurrect it.

Transantlantic Dialogue: Economic, Social and Economic Framework Policy

Issues of economic and social policy have always formed an integral part of the dialogue program of the KAS Washington. On both sides of the Atlantic, reform efforts in the fields of pension and health policy continue to be important and pressing issues. In the light of increasing budgetary constraints and the aging of society in both the U.S. and in Europe, the debates on the reform of the social security system will become increasingly more virulent in the future. In the U.S., especially against the backdrop of stable economic growth and a low unemployment rate, the issue of social justice is increasingly being raised in conjunction with wealth distribution ("income gap"). Immediately after the midterm congressional elections, the demand for a raise in the statutory minimum wages has moved to the top of the agenda of the Congress, which since the beginning of 2007 is dominated by the Democrats. Due to the record U.S. budget deficit this matter is expected to be a major election issue during the 2008 presidential election campaign. In addition, voices questioning the ecological responsibility of the U.S. will become louder and not fall on deaf ears in Congress. European and German economic policy is often severely criticized in the United States. In certain areas, European economic policy can benefit from U.S. experience, a case in point being the flexibility of the labor market. The Konrad Adenauer Foundation in Washington has organized several events focusing on such issues, and arranges a dialogue between politicians and experts from both sides of the Atlantic.

The relationship between religion and politics is another issue that is gaining increasing significance within the transatlantic dialogue. One reason for this is that the engagement with other cultures has resulted in growing interest and reflection on the values of the West as well. Another reason is that many European observers are partly fascinated and partly irritated by the role of religion in American politics. This issue played an important role in the last presidential elections as well as in the recent midterm congressional elections. There is no reason to believe that it will be otherwise in the forthcoming 2008 presidential election. Europe has to strive for a better understanding of this discussion and learn from it. Consequently, the Konrad Adenauer Foundation in Washington is promoting cooperation between evangelicals and other religious organizations by organizing conferences and arranging visits to Europe and the United States.

Internal developments in the U.S. during 2007 and 2008 will become exceedingly interesting due to the forthcoming presidential elections. The most important goal of the Konrad Adenauer Foundation in Washington is, therefore, to identify these developments as early as possible and to convey this information to Europe and Germany.

A Focused Exchange of Information as a Corrective to the Image of America in Europe

The Washington Office functions as a relay station or mediator for transatlantic target groups in the fields of politics, economics and science. It offers information and consultation services for in-house, foundation-specific political communication as well as for close partners of the KAS. The often one-sided reporting in the European media on political, economic and social developments in the U.S. continues to be a matter of concern. Conversely, it is equally true, that in the U.S. there is frequently little or incomplete and inadequate information available on European or German politics, economy and society in Europe. The Konrad Adenauer Foundation in Washington seeks to provide and disseminate appropriate information on both sides of the Atlantic through its consistently sound reporting and other measures. The KAS Washington has done pioneering work, for example in the run-up to the congressional elections, by creating a blog on the internet site of the Washington Office, which registered thousands of hits.

Multinational Dialogue on Development

The wide-ranging failure of U.S. intervention in Iraq highlights the pressing need on the part of the U.S. to evolve a new strategy in the Middle East. The victory of the Democratic Party in the midterm congressional elections in November 2006 has accelerated the search for such a strategy. It is becoming increasingly clear that it is not sufficient to win a war. Establishing peace is equally important. The use of military instruments has to be optimally coordinated with the use of instruments for creating and maintaining peace. The U.S. are hoping for a greater involvement of their partners and international organizations, especially that of the Europeans, more particularly the Germans, in tackling these challenges. In recent times American interest in the experience of Europeans with regard to nation-building, rule of law and the fostering of democracy etc. is clearly on the rise.

A corollary of this is the perceived need of the U.S. Administration to intensify the developmental dialogue with its European partners, especially Germany. The focus, here, is on promoting democracy rooted in the rule of law, nation-building and the development of a functioning economic system. There is, today, a widespread belief that the enormous challenges facing the Western industrialized nations globally can only be tackled and resolved jointly.

The success of the U.S. in this endeavor is also in the best interests of its partners in the West. Consequently, Germany must support and help in advancing the process of stabilization and development of democratic structures in these countries, particularly in the Middle East.

These issues played an extremely important role during the meeting of Chancellor Merkel with President Bush in Washington at the beginning of January 2007. The Quartet on the Middle East has been revived on the proposal of Chancellor Merkel with a view to ending the Israel Palestinian conflict. This was one of the first initiatives the Chancellor took in the context of the German EU Council presidency in the first half of 2007.

The fostering of democracy, rule of law and human rights and of viable economic development is also central to the international organizations located in the United States. The fight against corruption in developing countries is also an important task, especially in the context of the World Bank and the International Monetary Fund (IMF). The United Nations also has an important role to play in the creation and maintenance of peace. In this context, there has been intense criticism of the UN, especially by the United States. The UN has been accused of being ineffective and possessing an excessive and cumbersome bureaucracy. It has also been accused of failure in various regional conflicts, as in the case of Darfur, in Sudan but equally also with regard to the dispute with Iran over its nuclear program

For German and European politicians on fact-finding visits to the U.S., as also in the case of specialized discussions and transatlantic conferences, the Konrad Adenauer Foundation in Washington offers a platform for a transatlantic and multinational dialogue on development with representatives of the U.S. Congress, U.S. Administration, various international organizations and with experts from the field of development.

Moreover, the Konrad Adenauer Foundation managed to arrange a fact-finding visit for a delegation of American members of Congress to Germany. The KAS, thus, succeeded in involving U.S. politicians in the German-American and the European-American dialogue. The involvement of key advisors in the American Congress is an important part of the dialogue process with American politicians, given the fact that members of Congress rarely visit foreign countries. Keeping in mind the scope for influencing transatlantic policy-making, the role of congressional staffers in such an endeavor cannot be sufficiently emphasized . The traditional "Congressional Staffer Program," which brings together important advisors of the Bush administration, of Congress, of the Senate as well as of the Republican and Democratic Party headquarters with their counterparts in Germany, had to be deferred to spring 2007 due to the midterm congressional elections. After many years, for the first time, in 2006, the KAS, Washington once again brought together a delegation of political advisors of the Bundestag (the lower house of the German parliament) with political policy makers in Washington, while the former were on a fact-finding visit to America. Finally, for the period covered by the report, the Washington Office was very focused in integrating the members of the European Parliament in the dialogue process with American multipliers, particularly with the Congress and the administration.

Cooperation with Jewish Organizations

Fostering ties with U.S.-American Jewish organizations remains central to the activities of the Konrad Adenauer Foundation in Washington. The exchange program between the Konrad Adenauer Foundation and the American Jewish Committee, which celebrated its 25th anniversary in 2006, forms the core of the German-American/Jewish dialogue. In addition, the Washington Office sought to expand the dialogue with the American Jewish community, for example with the Jewish organization, B'nai B'rith, the Leo Baeck Institute and the Jewish Theological Seminary in New York.

This dialogue also contributes substantively towards consolidating and intensifying the cooperation between Europe and the United States. It helps in creating awareness about our shared values and common roots and in resolving common problems jointly.

The Main European Institutions: A Short Introduction

Falk-Ulrich von Hoff

I. The European Parliament

The Parliament's origins go back to the 1950s and the founding treaties. Since 1979, European Parliament's Members, or MEPs, have been directly elected by the citizens they represent.

Parliamentary elections are held every five years, and every EU citizen who is registered as a voter is entitled to vote. So Parliament expresses the democratic will of the Union's citizens, and it represents their interests in discussions with the other EU institutions.

In January 2007 Hans-Gert Pöttering was elected President of the European Parliament.

The European Parliament works in France, Belgium and Luxembourg.

The monthly plenary sessions, which all MEPs attend, are held in Strasbourg, France—the Parliament's "seat". Parliamentary committee meetings and any additional plenary sessions are held in Brussels, Belgium, while Luxembourg is home to the administrative offices (the "General Secretariat").

Parliament has three main roles:

1. It shares the power to legislate with the Council. The fact that it is a directly elected body helps guarantee the democratic legitimacy of European law.

2. It exercises democratic supervision over all EU institutions, in particular the Commission. It has the power to approve or reject the nomination of Commissioners, and it has the right to censure the Commission as a whole.

3. It shares with the Council authority over the EU budget and can therefore influence EU spending. At the end of the procedure, it adopts or rejects the budget in its entirety.

The power to legislate

The most common procedure for adopting EU legislation is "co-decision" (see the section on Decision-making in the European Union). This places the European Parliament and the Council on an equal footing. The laws passed using this procedure are joint acts of the Council and Parliament. These joint acts of Council and Parliament are applicable in a wide range of fields.

Parliament must be consulted on a range of other proposals, for its approval is required for certain important political or institutional decisions.

Parliament also brings new legislation by examining the Commission's annual work program; for in so doing, it considers the kind of laws that would be appropriate. When it finalizes its decision, it will request the Commission to put forward the relevant proposals.

Democratic supervision

Parliament exercises democratic supervision over the other European institutions in several ways. First, before a new Commission is to be appointed, Parliament interviews all the prospective new members and President of the Commission (who are nominated by the member states). The members of the Commission cannot be appointed without Parliament's approval. Second, the Commission is politically answerable to Parliament, which can pass a "motion of censure" calling for its mass resignation.

More generally, Parliament exercises control by regularly examining reports it receives from the Commission. These reports range from general report to reports on the implementation of the budget, the application of Community law, etc. Moreover, the MEPs regularly ask the Commission written and oral questions.

The members of the Commission attend Parliament's plenary sessions and meetings of the parliamentary committees, thus maintaining a continual dialogue between the two institutions.

Parliament also monitors the work of the Council. The MEPs regularly pose the Council written and oral questions, while the President of the Council attends the plenary sessions and takes part in important debates.

Parliament works closely with the Council in areas of common foreign and security policy and judicial co-operation, as well as issues of common interest such as asylum and immigration policy and measures to combat drug abuse, fraud and international crime. The Council Presidency keeps Parliament informed of all these subjects.

Parliament can also exercise democratic control by examining petitions from citizens and setting up temporary committees of inquiry.

Finally, Parliament provides input to every EU summit (the European Council meetings). At the opening of each summit, the President of Parliament is invited to express Parliament's views and concerns on the main topical issues as well as items on the European Council's agenda.

The power of the purse

The EU's annual budget is decided jointly by Parliament and the Council of the European Union. Parliament debates it in two successive readings, and it does not come into force until it has been signed by the President of Parliament.

Parliament's Committee on Budgetary Control (COCOBU) monitors how the budget is spent. Each year, Parliament decides whether to approve the Commission's handling of the budget for the previous financial year. This approval process is technically known as "granting a discharge".

Parliament's work is divided into two main stages:

1. *Preparing for the plenary session.* This is done by the MEPs in the various parliamentary committees specializing in particular areas of EU activity. The issues for debate are also discussed by the political groups.

2. *The plenary session itself.* Plenary sessions, attended by all MEPs, are normally held in Strasbourg (for one week per

> month) and sometimes in Brussels (two days). At these sessions, Parliament examines proposed legislation and votes on amendments before coming to a decision on the text as a whole.

Other items on the agenda may include Council or Commission "communications" or questions as to the on goings in the European Union or the wider world.

General Structure of the EP

The President oversees all the activities of Parliament and its constituent bodies. He presides over its part-sessions and chairs the meetings of the *Bureau and Conference of Presidents.* He represents Parliament in all external relations, particularly international relations.

In addition to the President, the *Bureau* includes the 14 vice-presidents and 6 quaestors (the latter in an advisory capacity). The Bureau is the regulatory body for the European Parliament. It meets twice a month to deal with financial, organizational and administrative matters concerning MEPs, the internal organization of the European Parliament, its secretariat and constituent bodies. In the event of a tied vote, the President has the casting vote.

The *Conference of Presidents* consists of the President of Parliament and the chairmen of the political groups. It is responsible for Parliament's political organization. It determines the organisation of Parliament's work and presides over matters relating to legislative planning. It manages relations with the other institutions and bodies of the EU as well as the national parliaments of member states. By extension, it is also responsible for maintaining relations with non-member countries and with non-EU institutions and organisations. It meets twice a month to set the agenda for the part-session. The part-session is a major prerogative because the European Parliament (unlike most national parliaments) has total sovereignty in setting its agenda.

The *5 quaestors* are responsible for administrative and financial matters relating directly to MEPs.

The *Conference of Committee Chairmen* coordinates the activities of the parliamentary committees. It makes recommendations to the Conference of Presidents as to the work of committees and the drafting of the part sessions' agendas.

The *Conference of Delegation Chairmen* may make recommendations to the Conference of Presidents as to the work of delegations.

The members of the *standing committees* in Parliament are elected during the first part-session of the newly elected Parliament (inaugural part session). New elections of these members are held every two and a half years. At their inaugural meetings, committees elect their bureau (a chairman and three vice-chairmen) by a secret ballot and without debate, for a term of two and a half years. In practice, nominations are made once the seats have been distributed amongst the political groups using the d'Hondt method. This method ensures that the balance of bureau members on committees and delegations reflects the distribution of seats in Parliament as a whole, in terms of political colour and nationality.

Standing committees may ask the Conference of Presidents for permission to appoint one or more *subcommittees* from among their members. The subcommittees do not vote on their own reports. Instead, their reports are considered by the parent committee that requested for its establishment. In other respects, the procedure for subcommittees is the same as that for committees. During the sixth parliamentary term, the subcommittee on security and defense and the subcommittee on human rights will assist the Committee on Foreign Affairs.

The Treaty of Maastricht makes it possible for one quarter of MEPs to set up a *temporary committee of inquiry*. The rules governing the exercise of this power of inquiry were decided in an inter-institutional agreement. As a result, it gave the European Parliament increased rights of access to documents.

The remit of a temporary committee of inquiry lasts for a maximum of one year, unless Parliament decides at the end of that period to extend it.

The committee instead of Parliament votes on the report of a temporary committee of inquiry. Once the report is adopted, the committee lays it before Parliament together with any minority opinions. If the committee requests it, the European Parliament may hold a debate on this report in the House. The committee is responsible for monitoring the action undertaken by the temporary committee of inquiry and, if appropriate, reports on it.

Delegations are set up to maintain relations with parliaments of non-EU countries or groups of non-EU countries. Unlike parliamentary committees they may not compile reports or table motions for resolutions before the House.

Members of the delegation bureaus are elected during the inaugural part-session, after nominations have been made to the Conference of Presidents by the political groups and Non-attached Members.

The Conference of Presidents appoints the other delegation members on nominations from the political groups and Non-attached Members. So doing ensures that there is a fair representation of Member States and political views. The political groups may designate a number of substitute members equal to the number of their group's full members. These substitute members attend delegation meetings, with no entitlement to vote, but they may not take part in delegation missions unless the full member is unable to travel.

Delegations meet less frequently than committees. Generally speaking they undertake a mission every other year in the country or countries for which they are responsible. In the year following a mission, they receive a delegation from the country concerned, usually in one of Parliament's customary places of work.

The Conference of Presidents has ruled that the MEPs may only take part in these missions if they have previously taken part in the preparatory meetings for them.

Parliament may set up *joint parliamentary committees* with the parliaments of states associated with the EU or states with which accession negotiations have been initiated. The powers and responsibilities of the various joint parliamentary committees and their rules of procedure are laid down in agreements with the non-EU countries concerned.

The membership of European Parliament delegations to joint parliamentary committees is determined in the same way as that of standing committees. They met at six-monthly intervals, alternately in the EP's customary venues for meetings and in the countries concerned.

The Cotonou Agreement between the European Community and the countries of Africa, the Caribbean and Pacific (the ACP countries) provides for the creation of a parliamentary institution called the ACP-EU *Joint Parliamentary Assembly*, consisting of an equal number of members of the European Parliament on the one hand and representatives of the ACP countries (one per country) on the other. This Assembly is a consultative body with powers of scrutiny and proposal. It has 154 members, 77 of whom are elected by the European Parliament using the same procedure as that used for setting up inter-parliamentary delegations. The Assembly is chaired by two co-presidents, one representing the ACP members and the other representing the European members.

Secretariat of the European Parliament

The European Parliament is assisted by a *Secretariat*. Some 4,000 officials recruited by open competition from all the countries of the Union and placed under the authority of a Secretary-General, work for the European Parliament.

The political groups have their own staff and the Members have parliamentary assistants.

The European Parliament is distinguished from other international organizations by its obligation to offer full multilingualism. Parliament works in all the official languages of the European Union – 22 since the enlargement in 2007. All documents handled by the plenary must be translated into all these languages.

The European Parliament also provides an interpretation service, so that every Member is able to speak in his/her mother tongue. This makes the European Parliament the world's largest employer of interpreters and translators, who account for one third of the institution's staff.

The *Secretariat* is located in Luxembourg and Brussels.

The *Secretary-General* is Parliament's most senior official. As his title implies, he heads the Secretariat. The Bureau determines the Secretariat's membership and organization. The Secretary-General is responsible for Parliament's administration. He is appointed by the Bureau.

II. The EPP-ED-Group

Since July 1999, the Group of the European People's Party (Christian Democrats) and European Democrats in the European Parliament has been the *largest political* group in the now 785-strong European Parliament.

277 Members of the European Parliament (MEPs) come from the EPP-ED Group. Thus, the EPP-ED Group represents some 35% of the total number of MEPs. The Group unites Christian Democrat, Conservative and other mainstream center and center-right political forces from across the 27-member European Union. The EPP-ED Group is the only one group in Parliament (out of the eight) whose MEPs are from all member states.

The Chairman of the EPP-ED Group is Joseph Daul, MEP. He chairs its governing body—a Presidency of eight Vice-Chairmen and a Treasurer—and speaks for the Group in keynote debates in the European Parliament. He is supported by coordinators on each of the Parliament's 24 committees and heads of the national delegations represented in the Group. The operational needs of the Group are serviced by a Group secretariat, which provides policy and organisational support. The Group runs its own think-tank, the European Ideas Network, which brings together opinion-formers from the worlds of politics, business, academia and civic society across Europe, to discuss the major policy issues facing the European Union.

Originally founded in June 1953 as the Christian Democrat Group in the embryonic Common Assembly of the European Coal and Steel Community (comprised of nominated members of national parliaments), the Group has been centrally involved in every stage in the history of the European Union, from its earliest beginnings to the current discussion of a European constitution.

Several parties represented in the EPP-ED Group also belong to the *European People's Party*, the first-ever transnational political party to be formed at European level. Others sit as allied Members of the Group. All work together to resist the political priorities of the left in Europe and to advance the goal of a building a more competitive and democratic Europe that will be closer to its citizens.

As the largest political group in a Parliament in which non-socialist parties now enjoy a clear majority, the EPP-ED Group is in strong position to set the political agenda and to win the most critical votes. Since 1999, the EPP-ED Group has been on the winning side of more votes than any other group in the European Parliament's monthly plenary sessions.

Strength of numbers also ensures that the EPP-ED Group Members hold a range of key positions within the Parliament—including the presidency of the Parliament and the chairmanships of nine of the EP's 24 committees or subcommittees. Within the parliamentary committees, EPP-ED Group Members are best placed to secure the right to author the EP's position on key pieces of draft legislation and other major reports. Indeed, the Group receives more rapporteurships on important subjects than any other group.

In seeking to maximize its influence, the EPP-ED Group has been able to draw on the fact that the European Parliament has become an increasingly powerful political institution within the European Union system.

Already given a right of co-decision with the EU Council of Ministers in many legislative fields by the 1993 Maastricht Treaty, the Parliament has seen the scope of joint law-making further widened by the Amsterdam (1999) and Nice (2003) Treaties. Today, it is an equal partner in the legislative process in over two-thirds of EU policy areas. In addition, it has the final say over the composition of non-agricultural spending and the appointment and dismissal of the European Commission.

Bodies of the EPP-ED-Group

The Chairman, together with the other members of the Presidency, is elected by secret ballot for a term of two and a half years. The successful candidate is the candidate who receives an absolute majority of votes cast by Group members in a first ballot or a simple majority of votes cast in a second ballot (he/she may stand for re-election).

The Group Presidency comprises the Chairman, assisted by a maximum of nine Vice-Chairmen including the Treasurer. Each Vice-Chairman has specific responsibilities: chairmanship of standing working groups, relations with the institutions, international relations, etc.

The Bureau of the Group comprises:

- the Presidency of the EPP-ED-Group,
- the heads of the national delegations and an additional member for every ten members of each delegation;
- EPP-ED members who are members of the EP Bureau
- EPP-ED chairmen of parliamentary committees,
- the EPP-ED coordinators on each of the parliamentary committees.

The main duties of the Bureau are:

- to prepare the strategic and political decisions of the Group,
- to formulate proposals concerning changes to the Group's Rules of Procedure and Financial Regulation,
- to prepare for the plenary sessions, highlighting the most difficult questions for the Group from the different national perspectives.

The Conference of the Group Presidency and heads of national delegations meet at least once a month (usually in advance of the Group's plenary assembly meeting, during the week of the Group's meeting in Brussels) to agree key guidelines of policy and prepare decisions of major importance for the Group's political strategy.

Full meetings of the Group, the *'Plenary Assembly'*, are held in the week preceding parliamentary part-sessions and during them. At these sessions, they consider:

- decisions on all political issues addressed inside and outside the EP,
- elections to the Group Presidency,
- appointment of members to fill the Group's seats in EP bodies,
- setting the Group's budget and approving the accounts,

- decisions on changes to the Group's Rules of Procedure and Financial Regulation.

The Plenary Assembly may always debate and set its agenda irrespective of the number of members present.

A quorum exists when the majority of the members of the Plenary Assembly are present.

Irrespective of the number of voting members present, decisions are valid provided the Chairman was not asked before the vote began to establish whether a quorum existed. If it is established that there is no quorum, the vote shall be postponed and placed on the agenda for the next meeting.

Unless the Group's Rules of Procedure provide otherwise, decisions shall be taken by simple majority.

The bodies of the Group (Presidency, Bureau) are re-elected and Group members are nominated afresh for governing functions within the EP (President, vice-presidents, quaestors, committee and delegation chairmen) at the beginning of each parliamentary term and midway through each term (every two and a half years). These functions are distributed amongst the political groups, and within the EPP-ED-Group, following negotiations which chiefly take account the applicants' personal qualities, the numerical size of the groups and national delegations, as well as the d'Hondt method of proportional seat distribution.

With a view to drafting and agreeing its political strategy and establishing voting guidelines, the EPP-ED-Group has five standing working groups within which it coordinates the work done by its members in the parliamentary committees. Each standing working group is headed by a chairman and two vice-chairmen. Working groups usually meet in Brussels the week before the part-session in Strasbourg and in advance of the meeting of the EPP-ED-Group's Plenary Assembly. Their job is to prepare and coordinate parliamentary work within the committees.

They also define the Group's position on the various agenda items for part-sessions, consider the initiatives (resolutions, questions, etc.) referred to them by the Group Presidency, and draw up the list of speakers for the Group in their areas of expertise.

Under the Group's Rules of Procedure, only members who have taken part in the vote at the committee stage and in the work of the standing working group may be allocated speaking time in Parliament.

EPP-ED-Group members belonging to the same parliamentary committee form a working group, which is coordinated by a coordinator who is elected by the members of this working group. Working groups meet ahead of the meetings of the parliamentary committees concerned, in order to prepare for them by drawing up voting lists and appointing rapporteurs and shadow rapporteurs.

The job of the coordinators and deputy coordinators is to coordinate work within their specific committee. To this end they hold preparatory meetings.

One or more technical advisers from the Group secretariat are made available to each committee and thus to each working group. With the help of these advisers the coordinator prepares for committee meetings, settles disputes by the requisite deadlines and takes the necessary action to ensure attendance at committee meetings.

When the committee addresses important or controversial issues the coordinator, with the help of the advisers, ensures that these issues are referred without delay to the appropriate standing working group or to the Group as a whole.

Members and substitutes who cannot attend a committee meeting must notify the advisers beforehand so that measures can be taken to ensure that the meeting proceeds smoothly vis-à-vis voting.

III. German Delegation

The German members of the European Parliament of the Christian Democratic Union (CDU) and the Christian Social Union (CSU) form the German delegation (German Group) of the European People's Party—European Democrats Group (EPP-ED). Making up 49 out of a total of 99 German members of the EP, the German Group is not only the largest German delegation in the EP but also the largest national delegation in the EPP-ED. Due to its size, the German delegation has a wider range of options for political actions as well as a higher degree of responsibility. Therefore, the German delegation strives to enforce the unity and the ability to act of the EPP-ED Group by assuring the other members (in particular the smaller national delegations) that their arguments and interests will be taken into account in the group-decisions of the EPP-ED. The solidarity within the EPP-ED regardless to the national and political background is an indispensable basis for the constructive co-operation in order to achieve their common goals.

The German delegation is led by a president from the CDU, a co-president from the CSU and a board of 5 vice-presidents, 2 whips and a treasury, all of them are members of parliament. It is the responsibility of the board to prepare sessions of the group, to execute decisions of the group and to represent the group in the conference of the board of the EPP-ED and the presidents of the national delegations on the one hand and to bodies outside the EP as far as main interests of the group are concerned on the other. Furthermore, the office of the board at Berlin organises the cooperation with the CDU/CSU Group in the German parliament, the German government, the mother parties and the political and social public in Germany.

In particular, the German delegation endeavors to reach an early coordination of the national institutions and bodies involved in European projects of legislation. In so doing, the quality of European legislation can be improved so much so that each member state would come to accept these supranational statutes.

The German members of the EP have the right to participate in the sessions of the different groups of the German parliament, as well as the European committee of the German parliament and of its working groups. As they may also present their arguments to these bodies, they are entitled to information by the German government. Moreover, there is continuous interaction and an exchange of information between the German delegation and the ministries of the German government.

This coordination and interaction aims to inform the national members of parliament, ministers and other decision-makers as well as opinion-makers in the media so as to reach the largest possible participation. Thus, they will be able to directly reach the voters.

European People's Party

The German members of the EPP-ED Group intensively participate in the work of the European People's Party.

A large majority of the parties in the EPP-ED Group belong to the European People's Party (EPP). The EPP is the first political party ever formed at European level. All EPP's member parties espouse centrist policies. While some of them have traditionally lent more towards Christian Democracy, the liberal and centrist wing is the strongest faction. The EPP-ED Group plays an active role in all EPP bodies. The current President of the EPP, Wilfried Martens, was chairman of the EPP Group during the 1994–99 parliamentary term; Secretary General Lopez Isturiz is also MEP.

The heads of government of the EU Member States attend every European Council meeting. Prior to each meeting of the European Council, the chairmen of the parties in the EPP meet at an 'EPP summit' to bring their respective views more closely in line. This ensures that they work together for the common good when discussing matters on the Council agenda. These meetings take place at least twice a year.

The European People's Party is a leading political group in other European forums, namely the Committee of the Regions, the Council of Europe, the Western European Union (WEU) and the Organization for Security and Cooperation in Europe (OSCE).

IV. The European Commission

The Commission is a politically independent institution, representing and upholding the interests of the EU. It is the driving force within the EU's institutional system. It proposes legislation, policies and programmes of action and is responsible for implementing the decisions of Parliament and the Council.

Like the Parliament and Council, the European Commission was set up in the 1950s under the EU's founding treaties.

The Members of the Commission are known as "Commissioners." They have all held political positions in their countries of origin, and many have been government ministers. But as Members of the Commission, they are committed to acting in the interests of the Union as a whole and not taking instructions from national governments.

A new Commission is appointed every five years, within six months of the elections to the European Parliament. The procedure is as follows:

- The member state governments jointly agree who is to be designated as the new Commission President.
- The Commission President-designate, in discussion with the Member State governments, chooses the other Commission members.
- The new Parliament then interviews and gives its opinion on the entire "college." If approved, the new Commission can officially start work the following January.

The present Commission's term started on November 24, 2004. Its current President is José Manuel Barroso.

The Commission is politically answerable to Parliament, which has the power to dismiss it by adopting a motion of censure. The Commission attends all the sessions of the European Parliament, where the latter must clarify and justify its policies. It also replies regularly to written and oral questions posed by MEPs.

The day-to-day work of the Commission is done by its administrative officials, experts, translators, interpreters and secretarial staff. There are approximately 24,000 of these European civil servants. That may sound a lot, but in fact it is fewer than the number of staff employed by most medium sized city councils in Europe.

Far from being faceless bureaucrats, these people are ordinary citizens from every EU country, selected through competitive examinations. Collectively, they are committed to building a strong and successful European Union.

The "seat" of the Commission is in Brussels, Belgium, but it also has offices in Luxembourg and representations in all EU countries and delegations in many capital cities around the world.

The European Commission has four main roles:

1. proposing legislation to Parliament and the Council;
2. managing and implementing EU policies and the budget;
3. enforcing European law (jointly with the Court of Justice);
4. representing the European Union on the international stage, for example by negotiating agreements between the EU and other countries.

Under the Treaty, the Commission has the "right of initiative". In other words, it is responsible for drawing up proposals for new European legislation. These proposals are, in turn, presented to Parliament and the Council. These proposals must defend the interests of the Union and its citizens rather than specific countries or industries.

Before making any proposals, the Commission must be aware of new situations and problems developing in Europe. In considering whether EU legislation is the best method forward, the Commission is in constant touch with a wide range of interest groups. It is obliged to consult two advisory bodies: the Economic and Social Committee (made up of employers' and trade unions' representatives) and the Committee of the Regions (made up of representatives of local and regional authorities). It also seeks the opinions of national parliaments and governments.

The Commission proposes action at EU level only if it believes that a problem cannot be solved more efficiently by national, regional or local action. This principle of dealing with things at the lowest possible level is called the "subsidiarity principle".

If, however, the Commission concludes that EU legislation is needed, then it drafts a proposal to effectively deal with the problem while encompassing a widest possible range of interests. To get the technical details right, the Commission consults the experts who make up its various committees and working groups.

As the European Union's executive body, the Commission is responsible for managing and implementing the EU budget as well as the policies and programmes adopted by Parliament and the Council. Despite the fact that most of the actual work and spending is done by national and local authorities, the Commission actually supervises the entire procedure.

One example of a policy actively managed by the Commission is competition policy. The Commission monitors cartels and mergers, and makes sure that EU countries do not subsidise their industries so much so that competition is distorted.

The Commission handles the budget under the watchful eye of the Court of Auditors. Both institutions aim to ensure good financial management. Only when it is satisfied with the Court of Auditors' annual report does the European Parliament grant the Commission discharge for implementing the budget.

The Commission acts as a "guardian of the Treaties". Thus the Commission works in conjunction with the Court of Justice to ensure that EU law is properly applied in all the member states.

If it discovers that a particular member state is not applying an EU law, and refusing to meet its legal obligations, the Commission takes steps to put the situation right.

If this procedure fails to put things right, the Commission refers the matter to the Court of Justice, which has the power to impose penalties. The Court's judgments are binding on the Member States and the European institutions.

The European Commission is an important mouthpiece for the European Union on the international stage. It enables the EU member states to speak "with one voice" in international forums such as the World Trade Organization.

The Commission also has the responsibility of negotiating international agreements on behalf of the EU. One well-known example is the Cotonou Agreement, which sets out the terms of an important aid and trade partnership between the EU and developing countries in Africa, the Caribbean and the Pacific.

It is up to the Commission President to decide which commissioner will be responsible for which policy area, and to reshuffle these responsibilities (if necessary) during the Commission's term of office. The President, with the Commission's approval, is also entitled to demand a commissioner's resignation.

The "college" of commissioners meets once a week, usually on Wednesdays in Brussels. Each item on the agenda is presented by the commissioner responsible for that policy area, and the college takes a collective decision on it.

The Commission's staff is organised into departments, known as "Directorates-General" (DGs) and "services" (such as the Legal Service). Each DG is responsible for a particular policy area and is headed by a Director-General. The Director-General is answerable to one of the commissioners. The DGs devise and draft the Commission's legislative proposals. However, these proposals only become official when it is "adopted" by the College at its weekly meeting.

A Commission with too many members would be unworkable. Until May 1, 2004, there were 20 commissioners—two from each of the most heavily populated member states and one from each of the other EU countries. However this was altered on November 1, 2004 when the 2004–2009 Commission took office, with 25 commissioners—one per country. As of January 1, 2007, when Bulgaria and Romania joined the Union, the EU has 27 member states, and 27 commissioners.

V. The Council of the European Union

The Council is the EU's main decision-making body. Like the European Parliament, the Council was set up by the founding treaties in the 1950s. It represents the member states. Its meetings are attended by one minister from each of the EU's national governments.

The agenda determines the ministers attending the respective meetings. If, for example, the Council is to discuss environmental issues, the meeting will be attended by the Environment Minister from each EU country and it will be known as the "Environment Council,"

The "General Affairs and External Relations Council" administers the EU's relations with the rest of the world. However, this Council configuration also has wider responsibility for general policy issues. Thus, its meetings are attended by whichever minister or state secretary each government selects.

Altogether there are nine different Council configurations:

1. General Affairs and External Relations

2. Economic and Financial Affairs ("ECOFIN")
3. Justice and Home Affairs
4. Employment, Social Policy, Health and Consumer Affairs
5. Competitiveness (Internal Market, Industry and Research)
6. Transport, Telecommunications and Energy
7. Agriculture and Fisheries
8. Environment
9. Education, Youth and Culture

Each minister in the Council is empowered to act for his or her government. In other words, the minister's signature is the signature of the whole government. Moreover, each minister in the Council is answerable to his or her national parliament and to the citizens that parliament represents. This ensures the democratic legitimacy of the Council's decisions.

The Council has six key responsibilities:

1. To pass European laws. It legislates jointly with the European Parliament in many fields.
2. To coordinate the broad economic policies of the member states.
3. To conclude international agreements between the EU and one or more states or international organizations.
4. To jointly approve the EU's budget with the European Parliament.
5. To develop the EU's Common Foreign and Security Policy (CFSP) according to European Council guidelines.
6. To coordinate cooperation between the national courts and police forces in criminal matters.

Much EU legislation is adopted jointly by the Council and Parliament. As a rule, the Council only acts on a proposal from the Commission. The Commission is normally responsible for ensuring that EU legislation, once adopted, is correctly applied.

The EU countries have decided that they want an overall economic policy based on close coordination between their national economic policies. This coordination is carried out by the economics and finance ministers, who collectively form the Economic and Financial Affairs ("ECOFIN") Council.

Each year, the Council "concludes" a number of agreements between the European Union and non-EU countries, as well as with international organisations. These agreements often cover broad areas such as trade, cooperation and development. Alternatively, it also deals with specific subjects such as textiles, fisheries, science and technology, and transport.

In addition, the Council may conclude conventions between the EU member states in fields such as taxation, company law or consular protection. Conventions can also deal with cooperation in the field of Justice and Home Affairs.

The EU's annual budget is decided jointly by the Council and the European Parliament. If the two institutions do not agree, the rules allow the Council to take the final decision on "compulsory expenditure" (mainly agricultural expenditure, and expenses arising from international agreements with non-EU countries), while Parliament has the last word on "noncompulsory" expenditure and the final approval of the budget as a whole.

The member states are developing a Common Foreign and Security Policy (CFSP). But foreign policy, security and defense are matters over which the individual EU member states retain independent control. They have not pooled their national sovereignty in these areas, so the European Parliament and the European Commission are able to play only a limited role. However, the EU countries have much to gain by working together on these issues, and the Council is the main forum in which this "inter-governmental co-operation" takes place.

To enable the EU to respond more effectively to international crises, the European Council (at the Helsinki summit meeting in December 1999) decided that the EU would create a "Rapid Reaction Force" of up to 60,000 military personnel that could be deployed within 60 days and kept in operation for at least a year.

New permanent political and military structures were established within the Council of the European Union by the European Council (Nice, December 2000) so as to provide political control and strategic direction in a crisis.

These new structures are:

- the Political and Security Committee (PSC)
- the European Union Military Committee (EUMC) and
- the European Union Military Staff (EUMS), composed of military experts seconded to the Council Secretariat by the member states.

In the area of Justice and Home Affairs closer cooperation is very important. Drugs, terrorism, international fraud, trafficking in human beings and the sexual exploitation of children are of great concern to European citizens. Cross-border cooperation is needed if these cross-border criminal activities are to be effectively tackled. If Europe is to do so, and give all its citizens equal access to civil justice throughout the EU, then the national courts, police forces, customs officers and immigration services of all EU countries have to work together.

They have to ensure, for example,

- that a court judgment delivered in one EU country in a divorce or child custody case is recognized in all other EU countries;
- that the EU's external borders are effectively policed;
- that customs officers and police exchange information on the movements of suspected drugs traffickers or people smugglers;
- that asylum seekers are assessed and treated in the same way throughout the EU, so as to prevent "asylum shopping".

Issues such as these, collectively known as "Justice and Home Affairs" (JHA), are dealt with by the Ministers for Justice and of the Interior, for they act collectively as the Justice and Home Affairs Council.

For the Council's work each EU member state has a permanent team in Brussels ("representation") that represents it and defends its national interest at EU level. The head of each representation is, in effect, his or her country's ambassador to the EU.

These ambassadors (known as "permanent representatives") meet weekly within the Permanent Representatives Committee (COREPER). The role of this committee is to prepare the work of the Council, with the exception of agricultural issues, which are handled by the Special Committee on Agriculture. COREPER is assisted by a number of working groups, made up of officials from the national administrations.

The Presidency of the Council rotates every six months. In other words, each EU country takes turns to be in charge of the Council agenda and chairs all the meetings for a six-month period, promoting legislative and political decisions and brokering compromises between the member states.

The Presidency is assisted by the General Secretariat, who prepares and ensures the smooth functioning of the Council's work at all levels.

In 1999, Javier Solana was appointed Secretary-General of the Council. He is also High Representative for the Common Foreign and Security Policy (CFSP), and in this capacity he helps to coordinate the EU's action on the world stage. Under the new constitutional treaty, the High Representative would be replaced by an EU Foreign Affairs Minister.

The Secretary-General is assisted by a Deputy Secretary-General. Together, they manage the General Secretariat.

Council decisions are taken by vote. The bigger the country's population, the more votes it has. But the number is not strictly proportional: it is adjusted in favour of the less populous countries.

As of January 1, 2007, the number of votes each country can cast (including the new member states) is as follows:

Germany, France, Italy and the United Kingdom	29
Spain and Poland	27
Romania	14
Netherlands	13
Belgium, Czech Republic, Greece, Hungary and Portugal	12
Austria, Sweden and Bulgaria	10
Denmark, Ireland, Lithuania, Slovakia and Finland	7

Cyprus, Estonia, Latvia, Luxembourg and Slovenia	4
Malta	3
TOTAL	345

The most common voting procedure in Council is "qualified majority voting" (QMV). This means that, for a proposal to be adopted, it needs the support of a specified minimum number of votes.

However, in some particularly sensitive areas such as CFSP, taxation, asylum and immigration policy, Council decisions have to be unanimous. In other words, each member state has the power of veto in these areas.

Unanimous agreement is already hard to achieve between 15 countries. In an enlarged Union of 27 or more, it will be virtually impossible. If it kept trying to operate under its present rules, the EU would be paralyzed – unable to act in many important fields. So the Treaty of Nice changes the rules, allowing the Council to take decisions by qualified majority voting in quite a number of areas that used to require unanimity.

As of January 1, 2007, a qualified majority has been reached

- if a majority of member states (in some cases a two-thirds majority) approve and
- if 255 votes are cast in favor—which is 73.9% of the total (roughly the same share as under the previous system).

In addition, a member state may ask for confirmation that the votes in favor represent at least 62% of the total population of the Union. If this is found not to be the case, the decision will not be adopted.

ANNEX

Institutions, Positions, Names, Addresses

Group I

European Parliament

Brussels
Rue Wiertz
B-1049 Brussels

Wiertzstraat
B-1047 Brussels
Tel.: +32-2-284 21 11 / +32-2-28 + extension
Fax: +32-2-284 69 74 / +32-2-230 69 33
Homepage: www.europarl.europa.eu

Luxembourg
Plateau du Kirchberg
B.P. 1601
L-2949 Luxembourg
Tel.: +352-43 00-1 / +352-43 00 + extension
Fax: +352-43 00 294 94
Homepage: www.europarl.europa.eu

Strasbourg
Allée dur Printemps
B.P. 1024/F
F-67070 Strasbourg Cedex
Tel.: +33-3 88 17 40 01 / +33-0-3 88 1 + extension
Fax: +33-3 88 25 65 01
Homepage: www.europarl.europa.eu

European Parliament Information Offices
Berlin
Unter den Linden 78
D-10117 Berlin
Tel.: +49-(0)30-2280-1000
Fax: +49-(0)30-2280-1111
E-Mail: epberlin@europarl.europa.eu
Homepage: www.europarl.de

München
Erhardtstr. 27
D-80331 München
Tel.: +49-(0)89-202 0879-0
Fax: +49-(0)89-202 0879-73
E-Mail: epmuenchen@europarl.europa.eu

Annex 1 Parliament's Bureau

POETTERING, Hans-Gert	President	EPP-ED
KRATSA-TSAGAROPOULOU, Rodi	Vice-President	EPP-ED
VIDAL-QUADRAS ROCA, Alejo	Vice-President	EPP-ED
ONESTA, Gérard	Vice-President	Greens/EFA
McMILLAN-SCOTT, Edward	Vice-President	EPP-ED
MAURO, Mario	Vice-President	EPP-ED
MARTINEZ MARTINEZ Miguel Angel	Vice-President	PSE
COCILOVO, Luigi	Vice-President	ALDE
ROTHE Mechthild	Vice-President	PSE
MORGANTINI Luisa	Vice-President	GUE/NGL
MOSCOVICI, Pierre	Vice-President	PSE
DOS SANTOS, Manuel António	Vice-President	PSE
WALLIS, Diana	Vice-President	ALDE
SIWIEC, Marek	Vice-President	UEN
BIELAN, Adam	Vice-Presidnet	UEN
NICHOLSON, James	Quaestor	EPP-ED
LULLING, Astrid	Quaestor	EPP-ED
DE VITS, Mia	Quaestor	PSE
FRIEDRICH, Ingo	Quaestor	EPP-ED
FAZAKAS, Szabolcs	Quaestor	PSE
MULDER, Jan	Quaestor	ALDE

Annex 2 Conference of Presidents

POETTERING, Hans-Gert	President	EPP-ED
DAUL, Joseph	Member	EPP-ED
SCHULZ, Martin	Member	PSE
WATSON, Graham	Member	ALDE
CROWLEY, Brian	Member	UEN
MUSCARDINI, Cristiana	Member	UEN
FRASSONI, Monica	Member	Greens/EFA
COHN-BENDIT, Daniel Marc	Member	Greens/EFA
WURTZ, Francis	Member	GUE/NGL
BONDE, Jens-Peter	Member	ID
FARAGE, Nigel	Member	ID
GOLLNISCH, Bruno	Member	ITS
BELOHORSKÁ, Irena	Member	NI

Annex 3 Parliamentary Committees

Parliamentary Committees: Internal Policies

on Budgets

on Budgetary Control

on Economic and Monetary Affairs

on Employment and Social Affairs

on the Environment, Public Health and Food Safety

on Industry, Research and Energy

on Internal Market and Consumer Protection

on Transport and Tourism

on Regional Development

on Agriculture and Rural Development

on Fisheries

on Culture and Education

on Legal Affairs

on Civil Liberties, Justice and Home Affairs

on Constitutional Affairs

on Women's Rights and Gender Equality

on Petitions

Parliamentary Committees: External Policies

on Foreign Affairs

Subcommittee on Human Rights

Subcommittee on Security and Defense

on Development

on International Trade

Temporary Committees

of Inquiry into the Collapse of the Equitable Life Assurance Society

on the alleged use of European countries by the CIA for the transport and illegal detention of prisoners

Annex 4 Chairmen/Chairwomen of the Committees

European Parliament
60, rue Wiertz / Wiertzstraat 60
B-1047 Brussels

Committee of Budgets	Chairman	**Reimer Boege** Bât. Altiero Spinelli, 15E169 Tel.: +32 (0)2 284 5326 Fax: +32 (0)2 284 9326 E-Mail: reimer.boege@europarl.europa.eu
Committee on Budgetary Control	Chairman	**Herbert Boesch** Bât. Altiero Spinelli, 15G254 Tel.: +32 (0)2 284 5677 Fax: +32 (0)2 284 9677 E-Mail: herbert.boesch@europarl.europa.eu
Committee on Economic and Monetary Affairs	Chairwoman	**Pervenche Berès** Bât. Altiero Spinelli, 14G206 Tel.: +32 (0)2 284 5777 Fax: +32 (0)2 284 9777 E-Mail: pervenche.beres@europarl.europa.eu
Committee on Employment and Social Affairs	Chairman	**Jan Andersson** Bât. Altiero Spinelli, 14G306 Tel.: +32 (0)2 284 5554 Fax: +32 (0)2 284 9554 E-Mail: jan.andersson@europarl.europa.eu
Committee on the Environment, Public Health and Food Safety	Chairman	**Miroslav Ouzký** Bât. Altiero Spinelli, 05F3656 Tel.: +32 (0)2 284 5810 Fax: +32 (0)2 284 9810 E-Mail: miroslav.ouzky@europarl.europa.eu
Committee on Industry, Research and Energy	Chairwoman	**Angelika Niebler** Bât. Altiero Spinelli, 15E254 Tel.: +32 (0)2 284 5390 Fax: +32 (0)2 284 9390 E-Mail: angelika.niebler@europarl.europa.eu
Committee on Internal Market and Consumer Protection	Chairman	**Arlene McCarthy** Bât. Altiero Spinelli, 13G218 Tel.: +32 (0)2 284 5501 Fax: +32 (0)2 284 9501 E-Mail: arlene.mccarthy@europarl.europa.eu

Committee on Transport and Tourism	Chairman	**Paolo Costa** Bât. Altiero Spinelli, 09G305 Tel.: +32 (0)2 284 5537 Fax: +32 (0)2 284 9537 E-Mail: paolo.costa@europarl.europa.eu
Committee on Regional Development	Chairman	**Gerardo Galeote Quecedo** Bât. Altiero Spinelli, 11E102 Tel.: +32 (0)2 284 5892 Fax: +32 (0)2 284 9892 E-Mail: gerado.galeote@europarl.europa.eu
Committee on Agriculture	Chairman	**Neil Parish** Bât. Altiero Spinelli, 14E206 Tel.: +32 (0)2 284 5392 Fax: +32 (0)2 284 9392 E-Mail: neil.parish@europarl.europa.eu
Committee on Fisheries	Chairman	**Philippe Morillon** Bât. Altiero Spinelli, 09G205 Tel.: +32 (0)2 284 5506 Fax: +32 (0)2 284 9506 E-Mail: philippe.morillon@europarl.europa.eu
Committee on Culture and Education	Chairman	**Nikolaos Sifunakis** Bât. Altiero Spinelli, 11G208 Tel.: +32 (0)2 284 5290 Fax: +32 (0)2 284 9290 E-Mail: nikolaos.sifunakis@europarl.europa.eu
Committee on Legal Affairs	Chairman	**Giuseppe Gargani** Bât. Altiero Spinelli, 09E206 Tel.: +32 (0)2 284 5168 Fax: +32 (0)2 284 9168 E-Mail: giuseppe.gargani@europarl.europa.eu
Committee on Civil Liberties, Justice and Home Affairs	Chairman	**Jean-Marie Cavada** Bât. Altiero Spinelli, 09G206 Tel.: +32 (0)2 284 5367 Fax: +32 (0)2 284 9367 E-Mail: jean-marie.cavada@europarl.europa.eu
Committee on Constitutional Affairs	Chairman	**Jo Leinen** Bât. Altiero Spinelli, 12G205 Tel.: +32 (0)2 284 5842 Fax: +32 (0)2 284 9842 E-Mail: jo.leinen@europarl.europa.eu

Annex 4 **Chairmen/Chairwomen of the Committees** ***(continued)***

Committee on Women's Rights and Gender Equality	Chairwoman	**Anna Záborská** Bât. Altiero Spinelli, 09E205 Tel.: +32 (0)2 284 5923 Fax: +32 (0)2 284 9923 E-Mail: anna.zaborska@europarl.europa.eu
Committee on Petitions	Chairman	**Marcin Libicki** Bât. Altiero Spinelli, 04F158 Tel.: +32 (0)2 284 5934 Fax: +32 (0)2 284 9934 E-Mail: marcin.libicki@europarl.europa.eu
Committee on Foreign Affairs	Chariman	**Jacek Saryusz-Wolski** Bât. Altiero Spinelli, 05F155 Tel.: +32 (0)2 284 5371 Fax: +32 (0)2 284 9371 E-Mail: jacek.saryusz-wolski@europarl.europa.eu
Subcommittee on Human Rights	Chairwoman	**Hélène Flautre** Bât. Altiero Spinelli, 08G130 Tel.: +32 (0)2 284 5364 Fax: +32 (0)2 284 9364 E-Mail: helene.flautre@europarl.europa.eu
Subcommittee on Security and Defense	Chairman	**Karl von Wogau** Bât. Altiero Spinelli, 10E206 Tel.: +32 (0)2 284 5301 Fax: +32 (0)2 284 9301 E-Mail: karl.vonwogau@europarl.europa.eu
Committee on Development	Chairman	**Josep Borrell Fontelles** Bât. Paul-Henri Spaak, 10B014 Tel.: +32 (0)2 284 5341 Fax: +32 (0)2 284 9341 E-Mail: josep.borrell@europarl.europa.eu
Committee on International Trade	Chairman	**Helmuth Markov** Bât. Altiero Spinelli, 06F349 Tel.: +32 (0)2 284 5980 Fax: +32 (0)2 284 9980 E-Mail: helmuth.markov@europarl.europa.eu

Annex 5 German Committee Members of the EPP-ED-Group

Committee	Member	Substitute
Committee on Foreign Affairs	Brok Gahler, Vice-Chairman Gomolka Posselt	Jarzembowski Konrad Lauk Pack Quisthoudt-Rowohl von Wogau
Subcommittee on Human Rights	Gahler	Posselt
Subcommittee on Security and Defense	von Wogau, Chairman	Ehler Konrad Radwan
Committee on Development	Posdorf Schroeder	Schnellhardt
Committee on International Trade	Caspary Quisthoudt-Rowohl, Vice-Chairwoman	Boege Dess
Committee on Budgets	Boege, Chairman Ferber Graessle	Gahler Gomolka Klamt
Committee on Budgetary Control	Ferber Graessle, Coordinator	Caspary
Committee on Economic and Monetary Affairs	Ehler Hoppenstedt Konrad Lauk Radwan, Coordinator	Goepel Langen Lehne Mann Schwab von Wogau
Committee on Employment and Social Affairs	Mann, Vice Chairman Stauner	Hieronymi Koch Liese Ulmer
Committee on the Environment, Public Health and Food Safety	Florenz Klass Liese Schnellhardt Ulmer Weisgerber	Hoppenstedt Nassauer Sommer
Committee on Industry, Research and Energy	Langen Niebler, Chairwoman Reul	Caspary Ehler

Annex 5 **German Committee Members of the EPP-ED-Group** ***(continued)***

Committee	Member	Substitute
Committee on Internal Market and Consumer Protection	Lechner Schwab, Vice-Coordinator	Niebler Posdorf Weisgerber
Committee on Transport and Tourism	Jarzembowski, Coordinator Koch Sommer	Ferber Gewalt Jeggle
Committee on Regional Development	Berend, Vice Chairman Pieper	Florenz Schroeder Weber
Committee on Agriculture	Dess Goepel, Coordinator Jeggle	Klass Mayer Pieper
Committee on Fisheries	Gomolka Jarzembowski	Boege Klamt
Committee on Culture and Education	Hieronymi Pack, Coordinator	Berend Graessle Posselt
Committee on Legal Affairs	Lehne, Coordinator Mayer Nassauer Wieland, Vice Chairman	Lechner Radwan Stauner
Committee on Liberties, Justice and Home Affairs	Gewalt Klamt Weber, Coordinator	Reul Wieland
Committee on Constitutional Affairs	Friedrich	Brok
Committee on Women's Rights and Gender Equality	Niebler Pack	Jeggle Klass
Committee on Petitions	Caspary Schwab Wieland,Vice-Coordinator	

Annex 6 Interparliamentary Delegations

Joint Parliamentary Committees (JPC)

Croatia
Delegation for relations with Switzerland, Iceland and Norway and to the European Economic Area (EEA)
EU-Former Yugoslav Republic of Macedonia (FYROM)
Turkey
Chile
Mexico

Parliamentary Cooperation Committees (PCC)

Armenia, Azerbaijan and Georgia
Moldova
Russia
Ukraine
Kazakhstan, Kyrgystan, Uzbekistan, Tajikistan, Turkmenistan and Mongolia

Interparliamentary Delegations

Delegation for relations with the countries of south-east Europe
Belarus
Israel
the Maghreb countries and the Arab Maghreb Union (including Libya)
the Gulf states (including Yemen)
the United States
the countries of Central America
Mercosur
the People's Republic of China
the countries of South-east Asia and the ASEAN
Australia and New Zealand
the Palestinian Legislative Council
the Mashreq countries
Iran
Canada
the countries of the Andean Community
Japan
the countries of South Asia and the SAARC
the Korean Peninsula
South Africa

Others

Delegations for relations with the NATO Parliamentary Assembly
Delegation to the Euro-Mediterranean Parliamentary Assembly (EUROMED)
Delegation to the EU-ACP Joint Parliamentary Assembly
Delegation to the Euro-Latin American Parliamentary Assembly (EUROLANT)

Annex 7 Chairmen/Chairwomen of the Interparliamentary Delegations

European Parliament
60, rue Wiertz / Wiertzstraat 60
B-1047 Brussels

Delegation for relations with Switzerland, Iceland and Norway and to the European Economic Area (EEA) +Switzerland, Iceland, Norway (SIN)	**Diana Wallis** Chairwoman Bât. Altiero Spinelli, 10G205 Tel.: +32 (0)2 284 5201 Fax: +32 (0)2 284 9201 E-Mail: diana.wallis@europarl.europa.eu
Albania, Bosnia-Herzegovina, Serbia and Montenegro (including Kosovo)	**Doris Pack** Chairwoman Bât. Altiero Spinelli, 10E102 Tel.: +32 (0)2 284 5310 Fax: +32 (0)2 284 9310 E-Mail: doris.pack@europarl.europa.eu
Russia	**Camiel Eurlings** Chairman Bât. Altiero Spinelli, 12E102 Tel.: +32 (0)2 284 5509 Fax: +32 (0)2 284 9509 E-Mail: camiel.eurlings@europarl.europa.eu
Ukraine	**Marek Maciej Siwiec** Chairman Bât. Altiero Spinelli, 12G305 Tel.: +32 (0)2 284 5653 Fax: +32 (0)2 284 9653 E-Mail: marek.siwiec@europarl.europa.eu
Moldova	**Marianne Mikko** Chairwoman Bât. Altiero Spinelli, 12G306 Tel.: +32 (0)2 284 5122 Fax: +32 (0)2 284 9122 E-Mail: marianne.mikko@europarl.europa.eu
Belarus	**Bogdan Adam Klich** Chairman Bât. Altiero Spinelli, 05F343 Tel.: +32 (0)2 284 5733 Fax: +32 (0)2 284 9733 E-Mail: bogdan.klich@europarl.europa.eu

Committees, and Delegation for relations with Tajikistan, Turkmenistan and Mongolia	**Ona Juknevicienе** Chairwoman Bât. Altiero Spinelli, 10G305 Tel.: +32 (0)2 284 5830 Fax: +32 (0)2 284 9830 E-Mail: ona.juknevicienе@europarl.europa.eu
Armenia, Azerbaijan and EU-Georgia	**Marie Anne Isler Béguin** Chairwoman Bât. Altiero Spinelli, 08H156 Tel.: +32 (0)2 284 5572 Fax: +32 (0)2 284 9572 E-Mail: marieanne.islerbeguin@europarl.europa.eu
Israel	**Paní Jana Hybášková** Bât. Altiero Spinelli, 12E206 Tel.: +32 (0)2 284 5519 Fax: +32 (0)2 284 9519 E-Mail: jana.hybaskova@europarl.europa.eu
Palestinian Legislative Council (PLC)	**Adamos Adamou** Chairman Bât. Altiero Spinelli, 06E240 Tel.: +32 (0)2 284 5964 Fax: +32 (0)2 284 9964 E-Mail: adamos.adamou@europarl.europa.eu
Maghreb	**Luisa Fernanda Rudi Ubeda** Chairwoman Bât. Altiero Spinelli, 11E242 Tel.: +32 (0)2 284 5268 Fax: +32 (0)2 284 9268 E-Mail: luisafernanda.rudiubeda@ europarl.europa.eu
Mashreq	**Béatrice Patrie** Chairwoman Bât. Altiero Spinelli, 13G130 Tel.: +32 (0)2 284 5883 Fax: +32 (0)2 284 9883 E-Mail: beatrice.patrie@europarl.europa.eu
Gulf States, including Yemen	**Lilli Gruber** Chairwoman Bât. Altiero Spinelli, 15G306 Tel.: +32 (0)2 284 5174 Fax: +32 (0)2 284 9174 E-Mail: lilli.gruber@europarl.europa.eu

Annex 7 **Chairmen/Chairwomen of the Interparliamentary Delegations** ***(continued)***

Iran	**Angelika Beer** Chairwoman Bât. Altiero Spinelli, 08H242 Tel.: +32 (0)2 284 5135 Fax: +32 (0)2 284 9135 E-Mail: angelika.beer@europarl.europa.eu
United States	**Jonathan Evans** Chairman Bât. Altiero Spinelli, 14E205 Tel.: +32 (0)2 284 5528 Fax: +32 (0)2 284 9528 E-Mail: jonathan.evans@europarl.europa.eu
Canada	**Seán Ó Neachtain** Chairman Bât. Altiero Spinelli, 04F361 Tel.: +32 (0)2 284 5611 Fax: +32 (0)2 284 9611 E-Mail: sean.oneachtain@europarl.europa.eu
Central America	**Raimon Obiols i Germà** Chairman Bât. Altiero Spinelli, 11G305 Tel.: +32 (0)2 284 5592 Fax: +32 (0)2 284 9592 E-Mail: raimon.obiolsigerma@europarl.europa.eu
Andean Community	**Alain Lipietz** Chairman Bât. Altiero Spinelli, 08G217 Tel.: +32 (0)2 284 5207 Fax: +32 (0)2 284 9207 E-Mail: alain.lipietz@europarl.europa.eu
Mercosur	**Achille Occhetto** Chairman Bât. Altiero Spinelli, 15G201 Tel.: +32 (0)2 284 5249 Fax: +32 (0)2 284 9249 E-Mail: achille.occhetto@europarl.europa.eu
Japan	**Georg Jarzembowski** Chairman Bât. Altiero Spinelli, 10E205 Tel.: +32 (0)2 284 5306 Fax: +32 (0)2 284 9306 E-Mail: georg.jarzembowski@europarl.europa.eu

People's Republic of China	**Dirk Sterckx** Chairman Bât. Altiero Spinelli, 10G306 Tel.: +32 (0)2 284 9111 Fax: +32 (0)2 284 9111 E-Mail: dirk.sterckx@europarl.europa.eu
South Asia, SAARC	**Neena Gill** Chairwoman Bât. Altiero Spinelli, 13G351 Tel.: +32 (0)2 284 5125 Fax: +32 (0)2 284 9125 E-Mail: neena.gill@europarl.europa.eu
Southeast Asia, ASEAN	**Hartmut Nassauer** Chairman Bât. Altiero Spinelli, 15E205 Tel.: +32 (0)2 284 5361 Fax: +32 (0)2 284 9361 E-Mail: hartmut.nassauer@europarl.europa.eu
Korean Peninsula	**Hubert Pirker** Chairman Bât. Altiero Spinelli, 08F136 Tel.: +32 (0)2 284 5766 Fax: +32 (0)2 284 9766 E-Mail: hubert.pirker@europarl.europa.eu
Australia and New Zealand	**Neil Parish** Chairman Bât. Altiero Spinelli, 14E206 Tel.: +32 (0)2 284 5392 Fax: +32 (0)2 284 9392 E-Mail: neil.parish@europarl.europa.eu
South Africa	**Lapo Pistelli** Chairman Bât. Altiero Spinelli, 09G306 Tel.: +32 (0)2 284 5587 Fax: +32 (0)2 284 9587 E-Mail: lapo.pistelli@europarl.europa.eu
NATO	**Paulo Casaca** Chairman Bât. Altiero Spinelli, 15G154 Tel.: +32 (0)2 284 5336 Fax: +32 (0)2 284 9336 E-Mail: paulo.casaca@europarl.europa.eu

Annex 7 **Chairmen/Chairwomen of the Interparliamentary Delegations *(continued)***

Croatia	**Pál Schmitt** Chairman Bât. Altiero Spinelli, 12E130 Tel.: +32 (0)2 284 5544 Fax: +32 (0)2 284 9544 E-Mail: pal.schmitt@europarl.europa.eu
EU-Former Yugoslav Republic of Macedonia (FYROM)	**Georgios Papastamkos** Chairman Bât. Altiero Spinelli, 08E210 Tel.: +32 (0)2 284 5448 Fax: +32 (0)2 284 9448 E-Mail: georgios.papastamkos@europarl.europa.eu
Turkey	**Joost Lagendijk** Chairman Bât. Altiero Spinelli, 08G305 Tel.: +32 (0)2 284 5176 Fax: +32 (0)2 284 9176 E-Mail: joost.lagendijk@europarl.europa.eu
Mexico	**Erika Mann** Chairwoman Bât. Altiero Spinelli, 12G342 Tel.: +32 (0)2 284 5191 Fax: +32 (0)2 284 9191 E-Mail: erika.mann@europarl.europa.eu
Chile	**André Brie** Chairman Bât. Altiero Spinelli, 06F343 Tel.: +32 (0)2 284 5403 Fax: +32 (0)2 284 9403 E-Mail: andre.brie@europarl.europa.eu
ACP	**Glenys Kinnock** Chairwoman Bât. Altiero Spinelli, 13G306 Tel.: +32 (0)2 284 5402 Fax: +32 (0)2 284 9402 E-Mail: glenys.kinnock@europarl.europa.eu
EUROLAT	**José Ignacio Salafranca Sanchez-Neyra** Chairman Bât. Altiero Spinelli, 11E206 Tel.: +32 (0)2 284 5603 Fax: +32 (0)2 284 9603 E-Mail: joseignacio.salafranca@europarl.europa.eu

Annex 8 German EPP-ED-Group Members in the Interparlamentary Delegations

Delegation	Member	Substitute
Delegation for relations with the countries of south-east Europe	Pack, Chairwoman	Koch Posselt
Croatia EU-Former Yugoslav Republic of Macedonia (FYROM)	Posselt Koch Mayer	Pack Goepel
Turkey	Langen Sommer, 3. Vice Chairwoman	Weber
Delegation for relations with Switzerland, Iceland and Norway and to the European Economic Area (EEA) + Switzerland, Iceland, Norway (SIN)	Goepel	Schwab Ulmer
Russia	Lehne	Stauner Weber
Ukraine		Gomolka Stauner
Moldova	Gomolka	Schnellhardt
Belarus	Gomolka	Berend
Committees, and Delegation or reslations with Tajikistan, Turkmenistan and Mongolia	Jeggle	Caspary Schnellhardt
Armenia, Azerbaijan and EU-Georgia	Stauner	Jeggle
Israel	Ferber	Reul
Palestinian Legislative Council (PLC)	Caspary	Hieronymi
the Maghreb countries and the Arab Maghreb Union (including Libya)	Pieper	Sommer
the Mashreq countries	Radwan, 1. Vice Chairman	Caspary
the Gulf states, including Yemen	Niebler Posdorf	
Iran	Friedrich	Gahler Lauk
the United States	Brok Lauk	Ehler Quisthoudt-Rowohl
Canada	Hieronymi	Boege

Annex 8 **German EPP-ED-Group Members in the Interparlamentary Delegations *(continued)***

Delegation	Member	Substitute
the countries of Central America	Liese	Schroeder
Mexico	Schroeder, 1. Vice Chairman	Liese
the countries of the Andean Community	Florenz Graessle	Hoppenstedt
Mercosur	Dess	Florenz Nassauer
Chile	Klass, 3. Vice Chairwoman	Weisgerber
Japan	Jarzembowski, Chairman	Lehne
the People's Republic of China	Hoppenstedt Reul	Langen Radwan
the countries of South Asia and the SAARC	Ehler Mann	Klamt Nassauer
the countries of Southeast Asia and ASEAN	Nassauer, Chairman	Poettering Posdorf von Wogau
the Korean Peninsula	Jarzembowski Quisthoudt-Rowohl Ulmer	Mayer
Australia and New Zealand	Boege Klamt	Pieper
South Africa	Gewalt	Gahler Niebler
ACP	Berend Gahler, 1. Vice Chariman Mayer Schnellhardt Schroeder Wieland	Dess Gewalt Graessle Klass Posdorf Quisthoudt-Rowohl Schwab Ulmer
EUROMED	Weisgerber	Ferber Friedrich Langen Lechner Radwan Schwab Sommer
NATO	von Wogau	Konrad
EUROLAT	Klass Liese Schroeder	

Annex 9 Members of the European Parliament by Political Group* and Country

6th term 2004–2009 (as of March 1, 2007)

	EPP-ED	PSE	ALDE	UEN	Greens/EFA	GUE/NGL	ID	ITS	(NI)	Total
Belgium	6	7	6		2			3		**24**
Bulgaria	4	6	7					1		**18**
Czech Republic	14	2				6	1		1	**24**
Denmark	1	5	4	1	1	1	1			**14**
Germany	49	23	7		13	7				**99**
Estonia	1	3	2							**6**
Greece	11	8				4	1			**24**
Spain	24	24	2		3	1				**54**
France	17	31	11		6	3	3	7		**78**
Ireland	5	1	1	4		1	1			**13**
Italy	24	15	12	13	2	7		2	3	**78**
Cyprus	3		1			2				**6**
Latvia	3		1	4	1					**9**
Lithuania	2	2	7	2						**13**
Luxembourg	3	1	1		1					**6**
Hungary	13	9	2							**24**
Malta	2	3								**5**
Netherlands	7	7	5		4	2	2			**27**
Austria	6	7	1		2			1	1	**18**
Poland	15	9	5	20			2		3	**54**
Portugal	9	12				3				**24**
Romania	9	12	9					5		**35**
Slovenia	4	1	2							**7**
Slovakia	8	3							3	**14**
Finland	4	3	5		1	1				**14**
Sweden	6	5	3		1	2	2			**19**
UK	27	19	12		5	1	10	1	3	**78**
Total	**277**	**218**	**106**	**44**	**42**	**41**	**23**	**20**	**(14)**	**785**

* Political groups: **EPP-ED**—Group of the European People's Party (Christian Democrats) and European Democrats; **PSE**—Socialist Group in the European Parliament; **ALDE**—Group of the Alliance of Liberals and Democrats for Europe; **UEN**—Union for Europe of the Nations Group; **Greens/EFA**—Group of the Greens/European Free Alliance; **GUE/NGL**—Confederal Group of the European United Left–Nordic Green Left; **ID**—Independence/Democracy Group; **ITS**—Identity, Tradition and Sovereignty Group; **NI**—Non-attached Members

Annex 10 Secretary-General

ROEMER Harald
E-Mail: harald.roemer@europarl.europa.eu

Annex 11 Cabinet of the President

WELLE Klaus
Head of Cabinet
PHS 11B062
60, rue Wiertz / Wiertzstraat 60
B-1047 Brussels
Int. Phone: Bru (32-2) 2846242
Int. Phone: Str (33-3) 88174831
E-Mail: klaus.welle@europarl.europa.eu

COLSMAN Johann Friedrich
Private Office of the President
PHS 10B012
60, rue Wiertz / Wiertzstraat 60
B-1047 Brussels
Int. Phone: Bru (32-2) 2841332
Int. Phone: Str (33-3) 88172783
E-Mail: johannfriedrich.colsman@europarl.europa.eu

RUHRMANN Katrin
Press, Speeches, Events
PHS 11B018
60, rue Wiertz / Wiertzstraat 60
B-1047 Brussels
Int. Phone: Bru (32-2) 2842573
Int. Phone: Str (33-3) 88174830
E-Mail: katrin.ruhrmann@europarl.europa.eu

Group II

Group of the European People's Party (Christian Democrats) and European Democrats

Annex 12 Members of the Presidency

DAUL Joseph,
Chairman
Bât. Altiero Spinelli
13E261
60, rue Wiertz / Wiertzstraat 60
B-1047 Brussels
Int. Phone: Bru (32-2) 2845525
Int. Phone: Str (33-3) 88175525
E-Mail: joseph.daul@
europarl.europa.eu

BONSIGNORE Vito,
Vice-Chairman
Int. Phone: Bru (32-2) 2845382
Int. Phone: Str (33-3) 88175382
E-Mail: vito.bonsignore@
europarl.europa.eu

HÖKMARK Gunnar,
Vice-Chairman
Int. Phone: Bru (32-2) 2845822
Int. Phone: Str (33-3) 88175822
E-Mail: gunnar.hokmark@
europarl.europa.eu

KARAS Othmar,
Vice-Chairman and Treasurer
Int. Phone: Bru (32-2) 2845627
Int. Phone: Str (33-3) 88175627
E-Mail: othmar.karas@
europarl.europa.eu

MARINESCU Marian-Jean,
Vice-Chairman
Int. Phone: Bru (32-2) 2845416
Int. Phone: Str (33-3) 88175416
E-Mail: marian-jean.marinescu@
europarl.europa.eu

MAYOR OREJA Jaime,
Vice-Chairman
Int. Phone: Bru (32-2) 2845601
Int. Phone: Str (33-3) 88175601
E-Mail: jaime.mayororeja@
europarl.europa.eu

NASSAUER Hartmut,
Vice-Chairman
Int. Phone: Bru (32-2) 2845361
Int. Phone: Str (33-3) 88175361
E-Mail: hartmut.nassauer@
europarl.europa.eu

PINHEIRO João de Deus,
Vice-Chairman
Int. Phone: Bru (32-2) 2845374
Int. Phone: Str (33-3) 88175374
E-Mail: joao.pinheiro@
europarl.europa.eu

STEVENSON Struan,
Vice-Chairman
Int. Phone: Bru (32-2) 2845710
Int. Phone: Str (33-3) 88175710
E-Mail: struan.stevenson@
europarl.europa.eu

SZÁJER József,
Vice-Chairman
Int. Phone: Bru (32-2) 2845871
Int. Phone: Str (33-3) 88175871
E-Mail: jozsef.szajer@
europarl.europa.eu

THYSSEN Marianne,
Vice-Chairwoman
Int. Phone: Bru (32-2) 2845918
Int. Phone: Str (33-3) 88175918
E-Mail: marianne.thyssen@
europarl.europa.eu

Annex 13 Heads of National Delegations of the EPP-ED-Group

Delegation	Number of Members	Heads
Federal Republic of Germany	49	Werner Langen Markus Ferber
United Kingdom	27	Timothy Kirkhope
Italy	24	Antonio Tajani Iles Braghetto
Spain	24	Jaime Mayor Oreja Gerardo Galeote
France	17	Margie Sudre
Poland	15	Jacek Saryusz-Wolski
Czech Republic	14	Jan Zahradil
Hungary	13	Józef Szájer Pál Schmitt
Greece	11	Ioannis Varvitsiotis
Portugal	9	Carlos Coelho Luís Queiró
Romania	9	Marian-Jean Marinescu
Slovakia	8	Peter Stástný
Netherlands	7	Camiel Eurlings
Austria	6	Othmar Karras Reinhard Rack
Belgium	6	Mathieu Grosch
Sweden	6	Gunnar Hökmark
Ireland	5	Avril Doyle
Bulgaria	4	Philip Dimitrov
Finland	4	Piia-Noora Kauppi
Slovenia	4	Mihael Brejc
Cyprus	3	Ioannis Kassoulides
Latvia	3	Valdis Dombrovskis
Luxembourg	3	Jean Spautz
Lithuania	2	Vytautas Landsbergis
Malte	2	Simon Busuttil
Denmark	1	Gitte Seeberg
Estonia	1	Tunne Kelam

Annex 14 EPP-ED-Group Coordinators in the Parliamentary Committees

Committee on Freign Affairs	José Ignacio Salafranca
Committee on Development	Maria Martens Nirj Deva
Committee on International Trade	Robert W. Strudy
Committee on Budgets	Salvador Garriga Polledo
Committee on Budgetary Control	Inge Gräßle
Committee on Economic and Monetary Affairs	Alexander Radwan
Committee on Employment and Social Affairs	Philip Bushill-Matthew
Committee on the Environment, Public Health and Food Safety	John Bowis
Committee on Industry, Research and Energy	Gilles Chichester
Committee on Internal Market and Consumer Protection	Malcolm Harbour
Committee on Transport and Tourism	Georg Jarzembowski
Committee on Regional Development	Lambert van Nistelrooij
Committee on Agriculture	Lutz Goepel
Committee on Fisheries	Carmen Fraga Estévez
Committee on Culture and Education	Doris Pack
Committee on Legal Affairs	Klaus-Heiner Lehne
Committee on Civil Liberties, Justice and Home Affairs	Manfred Weber
Committee on Constitutional Affairs	Inigo Mendez de Vigo
Committee on Women's Rights and Gender Equality	Amalia Sartori
Committee on Petitions	Robert Atkins
Subcommittee on Security and Defense	Stefano Zappata
Subcommittee on Human Rights	Simon Coveney

Annex 15 Secretariat of the EPP-ED-Group in the European Parliament

47-53, Rue Wiertz
B-1047 Brussels
Tel.: +32 2 284 2234
Fax: + 32 2 230 6208
E-Mail: epp-ed@europarl.europa.eu

Secretary-General
PEDERSEN, Niels
Tel. Bxl: +32-2284 3022
Tel. Strbg: +33-388 174879
E-Mail: niels.pedersen@europarl.europa.eu

BIESMANS, John
Deputy Secretary General
Tel. Bxl: +32-228 4 3026
Tel. Strbg: +33-388 1 74852
E-Mail: john.biesmans@europarl.europa.eu

Central Secretariat—Relations with Close National Political Groups, Parties, National Parliaments, Foundations, Religions
BILLER, Stephen
Tel. Bxl: +32-2284 3012
Tel. Strbg: +33-388 1 75117
E-Mail: stephen.biller@europarl.europa.eu

External Office Berlin
ARENS, Markus
Tel. Berlin: +49-30 227 75775
Tel. Bxl: +32-2284 2233
Tel. Strbg: +33-388 173034
E-Mail: markus.arens@europarl.europa.eu

Parliamentary Work
KAMP, Martin
Tel. Bxl: +32-228 4 3265
Tel. Strbg: +33-388 1 74419
E-Mail: martin.kamp@europarl.europa.eu

Parliamentary Work—Policy Strategy Unit, Legislative programme and European Ideas Network (EIN)
TEASDALE, Anthony
Tel. Bxl: +32-228 4 1678
Tel. Strbg: +33-388 1 72769
E-Mail: anthony.teasdale@europarl.europa.eu

Parliamentary Work—Working Group A
HILDEBRANDT, Arthur
Tel. Bxl: +32-228 4 2607
Tel. Strbg: +33-388 1 72744
E-Mail: arthur.hildebrandt@europarl.europa.eu

Parliamentary Work—Working Group B
REID, Alan
Tel. Bxl: +32-228 4 3027
Tel. Strbg: +33-388 1 73502
E-Mail: alan.reid@europarl.europa.eu

Parliamentary Work—Working Group C
KROEGEL, Werner
Tel. Bxl: +32-228 4 2565
Tel. Strbg: +33-388 1 74064
E-Mail: werner.kroegel@europarl.europa.eu

Parliamentary Work—Working Group D
SCRIBAN-CUVELIER, Natacha
Tel. Bxl: +32-228 4 2254
Tel. Strbg: +33-388 1 72254
E-Mail: natacha.scriban@europarl.europa.eu

Parliamentary Work—Working Group E
CALDEIRA DA SILVA, Catarina
Tel. Bxl: +32-228 4 3171
Tel. Strbg: +33-388 1 72713
E-Mail: catarina.caldeira@europarl.europa.eu

Press
GOELZ, Knut
Tel. Bxl: +32-228 4 1341
Tel. Strbg: +33-388 1 72797
Mobil: +32-479 972144
E-Mail: knut.goelz@europarl.europa.eu

International Relations—Delegations
HILDEBRANDT, Arthur
Tel. Bxl: +32-228 4 2607
Tel. Strbg: +33-388 1 72744
E-Mail: arthur.hildebrandt@europarl.europa.eu

USA
KROEGEL, Werner
Tel. Bxl: +32-228 4 2565
Tel. Strbg: +33-388 1 74064
E-Mail: werner.kroegel@europarl.europa.eu

Group III

German Delegation

Annex 16 Board of the German Delegation in the EPP-ED-Group

LANGEN, Werner (Chairman)
FERBER, Markus (Co-Chairman)
BOEGE, Reimer (Vice-Chairman)
EHLER, Christian (Vice-Chairman)
JEGGLE, Elisabeth (Vice-Chairwoman)
LIESE, Peter (Vice-Chairman)
PACK, Doris (Vice-Chairwoman)
GOEPEL, Lutz (Treasurer)
GRAESSLE, Ingeborg (Whip)
NIEBLER, Angelika (Whip)
LEHNE, Klaus Heiner

Annex 17 Members of the German Delegation

BEREND, Rolf
CDU
EPBrussels, ASP 10 E 169
Tel.: 00322/ 284 54 13
Fax: 00322/ 284 94 13
E-Mail: rolf.berend@europarl.europa.eu

BOEGE, Reimer
CDU
EPBrussels, ASP 15 E 169
Tel.: 00322/ 284 53 26
Fax: 00322/ 284 93 26
E-Mail: reimer.boege@europarl.europa.eu

BROK, Elmar
CDU
EPBrussels, ASP 10 E 130
Tel.: 00322/ 284 53 23
Fax: 00322/ 284 93 23
E-Mail: elmar.brok@europarl.europa.eu

CASPARY, Daniel
CDU
EPBrussels, ASP 15 E 101
Tel.: 00322/ 284 59 78
Fax: 00322/ 284 99 78
E-Mail: daniel.caspary@europarl.europa.eu

DESS, Albert
CSU
EPBrussels, ASP 15 E 246
Tel.: 00322/ 284 52 31
Fax: 00322/ 284 92 31
E-Mail: albert.dess@europarl.europa.eu

EHLER, Dr. Christian
CDU
EPBrussels, ASP 15 E 153
Tel.: 00322/ 2 84 53 25
Fax: 00322/ 2 84 93 25
E-Mail: janchristian.ehler@europarl.europa.eu

FERBER, Markus
CSU
EPBrussels, ASP 15 E 242
Tel.: 00322/ 284 52 30
Fax: 00322/ 284 92 30
E-Mail: markus.ferber@europarl.europa.eu

FLORENZ, KarlHeinz
CDU
EPBrussels, ASP 15 E 206
Tel.: 00322/ 284 53 20
Fax: 00322/ 284 93 20
E-Mail: karl-heinz.florenz@europarl.europa.eu

Annex 17 **Members of the German Delegation** *(continued)*

FRIEDRICH, Dr. Ingo
CSU
EPBrussels, ASP 15 E 102
Tel.: 00322/ 284 53 24
Fax: 00322/ 284 93 24
E-Mail: ingo.friedrich@europarl.europa.eu

GAHLER, Michael
CDU
EP-Brussels, ASP 10 E 217
Tel.: 00322/ 284 59 77
Fax: 00322/ 284 99 77
E-Mail: michael.gahler@europarl.europa.eu

GEWALT, Roland
CDU
EP-Brussels, ASP 15 E 258
Tel. 00322/ 284 54 42
Fax 00322/ 284 94 42
E-Mail: roland.gewalt@europarl.europa.eu

GOEPEL, Dr. agr. Lutz
CDU
EPBrussels, ASP 10 E 246
Tel. 00322/ 284 57 60
Fax: 00322/ 284 97 60
E-Mail: lutz.goepel@europarl.europa.eu

GOMOLKA, Prof. Dr. Alfred
CDU
EPBrussels, ASP 10 E 157
Tel.: 00322/ 284 53 07
Fax: 00322/ 284 93 07
E-Mail: alfred.gomolka@europarl.europa.eu

GRAESSLE, Dr. Ingeborg
CDU
EPBrussels, ASP 15 E 130
Tel.: 00322/ 284 58 68
Fax: 00322/ 284 98 68
E-Mail: ingeborg.graessle@
europarl.europa.eu

HIERONYMI, Ruth
CDU
EP-Brussels, ASP 15 E 261
Tel.: 00322/ 284 58 59
Fax: 00322/ 284 98 59
E-Mail: ruth.hieronymi@europarl.europa.eu

HOPPENSTEDT, Dr. Karsten Friedrich
CDU
EPBrussels, ASP 15 E 142
Tel.: 00322/ 284 56 60
Fax: 00322/ 284 96 60
E-Mail: karstenfriedrich.hoppenstedt@
europarl.europa.eu

JARZEMBOWSKI, Dr. Georg
CDU
EPBrussels, ASP 10 E 205
Tel.: 00322/ 284 53 06
Fax: 00322/ 284 93 06
E-Mail: georg.jarzembowski@
europarl.europa.eu

JEGGLE, Elisabeth
CDU
EP-Brussels, ASP 10 E 209
Tel.: 00322/ 284 53 51
Fax: 00322/ 284 93 51
E-Mail: elisabeth.jeggle@europarl.europa.eu

KLAMT, Ewa
CDU
EP-Brussels, ASP 15 E 146
Tel.: 00322/ 284 59 71
Fax: 00322/ 284 99 71
E-Mail: ewa.klamt@europarl.europa.eu

KLASS, Christa
CDU
EPBrussels, ASP 10 E 165
Tel.: 00322/ 284 53 13
Fax: 00322/ 284 93 13
E-Mail: christa.klass@europarl.europa.eu

KOCH, Dr. Ing. Dieter-Lebrecht
CDU
EPBrussels, ASP 10 E 258
Tel.: 00322/ 284 57 61
Fax: 00322/ 284 97 61
E-Mail: dieter-lebrecht.koch@
europarl.europa.eu

KONRAD, Dr. Christoph
CDU
EPBrussels, ASP 10 E 115
Tel.: 00322/ 284 53 33
Fax: 00322/ 284 93 33
E-Mail: christoph.konrad@
europarl.europa.eu

LANGEN, Dr. Werner
CDU
EPBrussels, ASP 15 E 158
Tel.: 00322/ 284 53 85
Fax: 00322/ 284 93 85
E-Mail: werner.langen@europarl.europa.eu

LAUK, Prof. Dr. Kurt-Joachim
CDU
EPBrussels, ASP 10 E 254
Tel.: 00322/ 284 57 72
Fax: 00322/ 284 97 72
E-Mail: kurtjoachim.lauk@
europarl.europa.eu

LECHNER, Kurt
CDU
EP-Brussels, ASP 15 E 253
Tel.: 00322/ 284 58 26
Fax: 00322/ 284 98 26
E-Mail: kurt.lechner@europarl.europa.eu

LEHNE, KlausHeiner
CDU
EPBrussels, ASP 10 E 103
Tel.: 00322/ 284 50 47
Fax: 00322/ 284 90 47
E-Mail: klaus-heiner.lehne@
europarl.europa.eu

LIESE, Dr. Peter
CDU
EPBrussels, ASP 10 E 158
Tel.: 00322/ 284 59 81
Fax: 00322/ 284 99 81
E-Mail: peter.liese@europarl.europa.eu

MANN, Thomas
CDU
EPBrussels, ASP 15 E 107
Tel.: 00322/ 284 53 18
Fax: 00322/ 284 93 18
E-Mail: thomas.mann@europarl.europa.eu

MAYER, Prof. Dr. Hans-Peter
CDU
EP-Brussels, ASP 15 E 154
Tel.: 00322/ 284 59 94
Fax: 00322/ 284 99 94
E-Mail: hans-peter.mayer@
europarl.europa.eu

NASSAUER, Hartmut
CDU
EPBrussels, ASP 15 E 205
Tel.: 00322/ 284 53 61
Tel.: 00322/ 284 67 02 (Assist. Bxl)
Fax: 00322/ 284 93 61
Fax: 00322/ 284 68 22 (Assist. Bxl)
E-Mail: hartmut.nassauer@
europarl.europa.eu

NIEBLER, Dr. Angelika
CSU
EP-Brussels, ASP 15 E 254
Tel.: 00322/ 284 53 90
Fax: 00322/ 284 93 90
E-Mail: angelika.niebler@europarl.europa.eu

PACK, Doris
CDU
EPBrussels, ASP 10 E 102
Tel.: 00322/ 284 53 10
Fax: 00322/ 284 93 10
E-Mail: doris.pack@europarl.europa.eu

PIEPER, Dr. Markus
CDU
EPBrussels, ASP 15 E 217
Tel.: 00322/ 284 53 05
Fax: 00322/ 284 93 05
E-Mail: markus.pieper@europarl.europa.eu

POETTERING, Prof. Dr. HansGert
CDU
EPBrussels, ASP 5 H 361
Tel.: 00322/ 284 57 69
Fax: 00322/ 284 97 69
E-Mail: hans-gert.poettering@
europarl.europa.eu

POSDORF, Prof. Dr. Horst
CDU
EPBrussels, ASP 10 E 210
Tel.: 00322/ 284 55 67
Fax: 00322/ 284 95 67
E-Mail: horst.posdorf@europarl.europa.eu

POSSELT, Bernd
CSU
EPBrussels, ASP 10 E 261
Tel.: 00322/ 284 52 32
Fax: 00322/ 284 92 32
E-Mail: bernd.posselt@europarl.europa.eu

Annex 17 **Members of the German Delegation** ***(continued)***

QUISTHOUDTROWOHL, Dr. Godelieve
CDU
EPBrussels, PHS 08 B 003
Tel.: 00322/ 284 53 38
Fax: 00322/ 284 93 38
E-Mail: godelieve.quisthoudt-rowohl@europarl.europa.eu

RADWAN, Alexander
CSU
EP-Brussels, ASP 15 E 218
Tel.: 00322/ 284 55 38
Fax: 00322/ 284 95 38
E-Mail: alexander.radwan@europarl.europa.eu

REUL, Herbert
CDU
EPBrussels, ASP 10 E 142
Tel.: 00322/ 284 52 44
Fax: 00322/ 284 92 44
E-Mail: herbert.reul@europarl.europa.eu

SCHNELLHARDT, Dr. Horst
CDU
EPBrussels, ASP 15 E 115
Tel.: 00322/ 284 56 18
Fax: 00322/ 284 96 18
E-Mail: horst.schnellhardt@europarl.europa.eu

SCHROEDER, Juergen
CDU
EPBrussels, ASP 15 E 157
Tel.: 00322/ 284 55 60
Fax: 00322/ 284 95 60
E-Mail: juergen.schroeder@europarl.europa.eu

SCHWAB, Dr. Andreas
CDU
EPBrussels, ASP 10 E 116
Tel.: 00322/ 284 59 38
Fax: 00322/ 284 99 38
E-Mail: andreas.schwab@europarl.europa.eu

SOMMER, Dr. Renate
CDU
EP-Brussels, ASP 10 E 154
Tel.: 00322/ 284 53 83
Fax: 00322/ 284 93 83
E-Mail: renate.sommer@europarl.europa.eu

STAUNER, Dr. Gabriele
CSU
EPBrussels, ASP 10 E 153
Tel.: 00322/ 284 57 11
Fax: 00322/ 284 97 11
E-Mail: gabriele.stauner@europarl.europa.eu

ULMER, Dr. Thomas
CDU
EPBrussels, ASP 15 E 116
Tel.: 00322/ 284 53 14
Fax: 00322/ 284 93 14
E-Mail: thomas.ulmer@europarl.europa.eu

WEBER, Manfred
CSU
EPBrussels, ASP 15 E 209
Tel.: 00322/ 284 58 90
Fax: 00322/ 284 98 90
E-Mail: manfred.weber@europarl.europa.eu

WEISGERBER, Dr. Anja
CSU
EPBrussels, ASP 15 E 210
Tel.: 00322/ 284 53 37
Fax: 00322/ 284 93 37
E-Mail: anja.weisgerber@europarl.europa.eu

WIELAND, Rainer
CDU
EP-Brussels, ASP 10 E 242
Tel.: 00322/ 284 55 45
Fax: 00322/ 284 95 45
E-Mail: rainer.wieland@europarl.europa.eu

WOGAU, Dr. Karl von
CDU
EPBrussels, ASP 10 E 206
Tel.: 00322/ 284 53 01
Fax: 00322/ 284 93 01
E-Mail: karl.vonwogau@europarl.europa.eu

Group IV

European Commission

Annex 18 The Members of the Barroso Commission (2004–2009)

European Commission
200, rue de la Loi
B - 1049 Brussels
Belgium
Tel.: +32-2 299 11 11 & CENTRAL
Homepage: http://www.ec.europa.eu

Commissioner	Ressort	E-Mail
BARROSO, José Manuel	President	jose-manuel.marroso@ec.europa.eu
WALLSTROEM, Margot	Vice President Institutional Relations and Communications Strategy	margot.wallstrom@ec.europa.eu
VERHEUGEN, Guenter	Vice President Enterprise and Industry	guenter.verheugen@ec.europa.eu
BARROT, Jacques	Vice President Transport	jacques.barrot@ec.europa.eu
KALLAS, Siim	Vice President Administrative Affairs, Audit and Anti-Faud	siim.kallas@ec.europa.eu
FRATTINI, Franco	Justice, Freedom and Security	franco.frattini@ec.europa.eu
REDING, Viviane	Information Society and Media	viviane.reding@ec.europa.eu
DIMAS, Stavros	Environment	stavros.dimas@ec.europa.eu
ALMUNIA, Joaquin	Economic and Monetary Affairs	joaquin.almunia@ec.europa.eu
HUEBNER, Danuta	Regional Policy	danuta.huebner@ec.europa.eu
BORG, Joe	Fisheries and Maritime Affairs	joe.borg@ec.europa.eu
GRYBAUSKAITÉ, Dalia	Financial Programming and Budget	dalia.grybauskaite@ec.europa.eu

Annex 18 **The Members of the Barroso Commission (2004–2009)** *(continued)*

Commissioner	Ressort	E-Mail
POTOCNIK, Janez	Science and Research	janez.potocnik@ec.europa.eu
FIGEL, Jan	Education, Training, Culture, and Multilingualism	jan.figel@ec.europa.eu
KYPRIANOU, Markos	Health and Consumer Protection	markos.kyprianou@ec.europa.eu
REHN, Olli	Enlargement	olli.rehn@ec.europa.eu
MICHEL, Louis	Development and Humanitarian Aid	louis.michel@ec.europa.eu
KOVÁCS, László	Taxation and Customs Union	laszlo.kovacs@ec.europa.eu
KROES, Neelie	Competition	neelie.kroes@ec.europa.eu
FISCHER BOEL, Mariann	Agriculture and Rural Development	mariann.fischer-boel@ec.europa.eu
FERRERO-WALDNER, Benita	External Relations and European Neighbourhood Policy	benita.ferrero-waldner@ ec.europa.eu
MCCREEVY, Charlie	Internal Market and Services	charlie.mc-creevy@ec.europa.eu
SPIDLA, Vladimir	Employment, Social Affairs and Equal Opportunities	vladimir.spidla@ec.europa.eu
MANDELSON, Peter	Trade	peter.mandelson@ec.europa.eu
PIEBALGS, Andris	Energy	andris.piebalgs@ec.europa.eu
KUNEVA, Meglena	Consumer Protection	meglena-shtilianova.kuneva@ ec.europa.eu
ORBAN, Leonard	Multilingualism	leonard.orban@ec.europa.eu

Annex 19 Secretariat-General

B-1049 Brussels
Tel.: (32-2) 299 11 11 &CENTRAL;
Int. Tel.: (32-2) 29 + extension
Telex: 21877 COMEU B
E-Mail: sg-info@ec.europa.eu

DAY, Catherine
Secretary-General
Tel.: 58312
E-Mail: catherine.day@ec.europa.eu

Legal Service
PETITE, Michel
Director-General
Int. Tel.: 65052
E-Mail: michel.petite@ec.europa.eu

Communication
SØRENSEN, Claus Haugaard
Director-General
Int. Tel.: 60393, 61684
E-Mail: press-web@ec.europa.eu

Economic and Financial Affairs DG
REGLING, Klaus
Director-General
Int. Tel.: 94366, 94360
E-Mail: klaus.regling@ec.europa.eu

Enterprise DG
ZOUREK, Heinz
Director-General
Int. Tel.: 94396, 51258
E-Mail: heinz.zourek@ec.europa.eu

Competition DG
LOWE, Philip
Director-General
Int. Tel.: 65040, 54562
E-Mail: philip.lowe@ec.europa.eu

Employment and Social Affairs DG
VAN DER PAS, Nikolaus
Director-General
Int. Tel.: 68308
E-Mail: nicolaus.van-der-pas@
ec.europa.eu

Agriculture DG
DEMARTY, Jean Luc
Director-General
Int. Tel.: 51910, 53274
E-Mail: jean-luc.demarty@ec.europa.eu

Energy and Transport DG
RUETE, Matthias
Director-General
Int. Tel.: 51992, 65002
E-Mail: matthias.ruete@ec.europa.eu

Environment DG
CARL, Mogens Peter
Director-General
Int. Tel.: 92205
E-Mail: mogens-peter.carl@ec.europa.eu

Research DG
SILVA RODRIGUES, José Manuel
Director-General
Int. Tel.: 58220
E-Mail: jose-manuel.silva-rodirgeus@
ec.europa.eu

Fisheries and Maritime Affairs DG
HOLMQUIST, Joergen
Director-General
Int. Tel.: 55192, 65192
E-Mail: joergen.holmquist@
ec.europa.eu

Internal Market and Services DG
STOLL, Thierry
acting-Director-General
Int. Tel.: 52387, 58819
E-Mail: thierry.stoll@ec.europa.eu

Taxation and Customs Union DG
VERRUE, Robert
Director-General
Int. Tel.: 54376, 60264
E-Mail: robert.verrue@ec.europa.eu

Education and Culture DG
QUINTIN, Odile
Director-General
Int. Tel.: 92277, 91960
E-Mail: odile.quintin@ec.europa.eu

Annex 19 **Secretariat-General** *(continued)*

Health and Consumer Protection DG
MADELIN, Robert
Director-General
Int. Tel.: 63338, 99090
E-Mail: robert.madelin@ec.europa.eu

Justice, Freedom and Security DG
FAULL, Jonathan
Director-General
Int. Tel.: 58658, 86269
E-Mail: jonathan.faull@ec.europa.eu t

External Relations DG
LANDABURU, Eneko
Director-General
Int. Tel.: 51968, 62211
E-Mail: eneko.landaburu@ec.europa.eu

Trade DG
O'SULLIVAN, David
Director-General
Int. Tel.: 92205, 94006
E-Mail: sg-info@ec.europa.eu

Development DG
MANSERVISI, Stefano
Deputy Director-General
Int. Tel.: 93238, 93237
E-Mail: stefano.manservisi@ec.europa.eu

Europe Aid-Cooperation Office
RICHELLE, Koos
Director-General
Int. Tel.: 63638
E-Mail: jacobus.richelle@ec.europa.eu

Directorate D—Asia
MULLER, Erich Wilhelm
Director
Int. Tel.: 90775
E-Mail: erich-wilhelm.muller@ec.europa.eu

Directorate B—Latin America
CARDESA GARCIA, Fernando
Int. Tel.: 92329
E-Mail: Fernando.cardesa-garcia@ec.europa.eu

Humanitarian Aid Office—ECHO
CAVACO, António
Director-General
Int. Tel.: 56711, 54249
E-Mail: antonio.cavaco@ec.europa.eu

Asia Central and South America
KENTRSCHYNSKYJ, Esko
Head of Unit
Int. Tel.. 53420
E-Mail: esko.kentrschynskyj@ec.europa.eu

Enlargement DG
LEIGH, Michael
Director-General (acting)
Int. Tel.: 58236
E-Mail: michael.leigh@ec.europa.eu

Budget DG
ROMERO REQUENA, Luis
Director-General
Int. Tel.: 95150, 53771
E-Mail: luis.romero-requena@ec.europa.eu

Joint Research Centre
SCHENKEL, Roland
Director-General
Int. Tel.: 99840, 61490
E-Mail: roland.schenkel@ec.europa.eu

European Anti-Fraud Office
BRUENER, Franz-Hermann
Director-General
Int. Tel.: 69063, 50327
E-Mail: franz-bruener@ec.europa.eu

Eurostat
CARRÉ, Hervé
Director-General
Int. Tel.: 62942
E-Mail: herve.carre@ec.europa.eu

Regional Policy
MEADOWS, Graham
Director-General
Int. Tel.: 56181, 66787
E-Mail: graham.meadows@ec.europa.eu

Annex 20 External Delegation in the United States

2300 M Street,NW
Washington, DC 20037
Tel.: (+202) 862 9500
Fax: (+202) 429 1766
E-Mail: relax-delusw-help@cec.eu.int

BRUTON, John
Ambassador, Head of Delegation

Group V

Council of the European Union

Rue de la Loi, 175
B – 1048 Brussels
Tel.: (32-2) 281 61 11
Fax: (32-2) 281 73 97
E-Mail: public.info@consilium.europa.eu

Secretary General of the Council of the EU and EU High Representative for the Common Foreign and Security Policy

SOLANA MADARIAGA, Javier

Press and current information
Tel.: (32-2) 281 63 19
Fax: (32-2) 281 80 26 / 85 41
E-Mail: press.office@consilium.europa.eu

Group VI

European Institutions, Agencies and Other Bodies

European Ombudsman
DIAMANDOUROS P. Nikiforos
1, av. du Président Robert Schumann
F-67001 Strasbourg Cedex
Phone: (33) 388 17 23 13
Fax: (33) 388 17 90 62
E-Mail: nikiforos.diamandouros@
ombudsman.europa.eu
Internet: http://www.ombudsman.europa.eu

European Economic and Social Committee
Rue Belliard 99
B-1040 Brussels
Phone: (32-2) 546 90 11
Fax: (32-2) 513 48 93
Internet: http://eesc.europa.eu

President
DIMITRIADIS, Dimitris

President's Cabinet
HAYDER, Roberto
Head of private office
Phone: (32-2) 546 97 41
Fax: (32-2) 546 97 52

Secretary-General
VENTURINI, Patrick
Secretary-General
Phone: (32-2) 546 93 52
Fax: (32-2) 546 97 53

Committee of the Regions
Rue Belliard 101
B-1040 Brussels
Phone: (32-2) 282 22 11
Fax: (32-2) 282 23 25
E-Mail: visitescdr@cor.europa.eu

President
DELEBARRE, Michel

Secretary-General
STAHL, Gerhard
Phone: (32-2) 282 20 05
Fax: (32-2) 282 20 07

Court of Justice of the European Community
Boulevard Konrad Adenauer
L-2925 Luxembourg
Phone: (352) 43 03-1
Fax: (352) 43 03-2600
Telex: 2771 CJINFO LU
E-Mail: info@curia.europa.eu
Internet: http://www.curia.europa.eu

President of the Court of Justice
SKOURIS, Vassilios

President of the Court of First Instance
VESTERDORG, Bo

European Data Protection Supervisor
Rue Wiertz, 60
B-1047 Brussels
Tel.: (32-2) 28 31 900
Fax: (32-2) 28 31 950
E-Mail: edps@edps.europa.eu

European Data Protection Supervisor
HUSTINX, Peter

Deputy Supervisor
BAYO DELGADO, Joaquín

European Central Bank
Eurotower
Kaiserstrasse 29
D-60311 Frankfurt am Main
Germany
Tel: (49-69) 13 44-0
Fax: (49-69) 13 44 60 00
Telex: 411 144 ecb d
E-Mail: info@ecb.int
Internet: http://www.ecb.int

President
TRICHET, Jean-Claude

European Court of Auditors
12, rue Alcide De Gasperi
L-1615 Luxembourg
Tel: (352) 43 98-1
Fax: (352) 43 98 46 430
E-Mail: euraud@eca.europa.eu
Internet: http://www.eca.europa.eu

VI. European Institutions, Agencies and other bodies *(continued)*

President
WEBER, Hubert
Phone: (352) 43 98-45592
Fax: (352) 43 98-46818

European Investment Bank
100, boulevard Konrad Adenauer
L-2950 Luxembourg
Phone: (352) 43 79-1
Fax: (352) 43 77 04
E-Mail: info@eib.europa.eu
Internet: http://www.eib.europa.eu

Board of Governors
Chairman
COWEN, Brian

European Investment Fund
43, avenue J. F. Kennedy
L-2968 Luxembourg
Phone: (352) 42 66 88-1
Fax: (352) 42 66 88-200
E-Mail: info@eif.org
Internet: http://www.eif.org

Chief Executive
CARPENTER, Francis

Eurojust
Maasweg 174
2516 AB The Hague
The Netherlands
Tel. +31-70 412 50 00
Fax: +31-70 412 55 55
E-Mail: info@eurojust.europa.eu
Homepage: www.eurojust.europa.eu

President of the College
KENNEDY, Michael

European Police Office (Europol)
Raamweg 47
2596 LW The Hague
The Netherlands
Tel. +31-70 302 50 00
Fax: +31-70 345 58 96
E-Mail: info@europol.europa.eu
Homepage: www.europol.europa.eu

Director
RATZEL, Max-Peter

Office for Harmonisation in the Internal Market (Trade Marks and Designs)
Avenida de Europa, 4
E-03008 Alicante
Spain
Tel. +34-965 13 91 00
Fax: +34-965 13 91 73
E-Mail: information@oami.europa.eu
Homepage: www.oami.europa.eu

President
DE BOER, Wubbo

European Environment Agency
Kongens Nytorv 6
DK-1050 København
Tel.: (45) 33 36 71 00
Fax: (45) 33 36 71 99
E-Mail: eea@eea.europa.eu
Homepage: www.eea.europa.eu

Executive Director
McGLADE, Jaqueline
E-Mail: Jacqueline.Mcglade@eea.europa.eu

European Food Safety Authority
Palazzo Ducale
Parco Ducale 3
I-43100 Parma
Italy
Tel.: (39) 05 21 03 61 11
Fax: (39) 05 21 03 61 10
E-Mail: info@efsa.europa.eu
Homepage: www.efsa.europa.eu

Executive Director
GESLAIN-LANÉELLE, Catherine
E-Mail: Catherine.geslain-laneelle@efsa.europa.eu

European Agency for Reconstruction
Egnatia 4
54626 Thessaloniki
Greece
Tel.: (30) 23 10 50 51 00
Fax: (30) 23 10 50 51 72
E-Mail: info@ear.europa.eu
Homepage: www.ear.europa.eu

Director
ZINK, Richard

European Agency for Safety and Health at Work
Gran Vía 33
48009 Bilbao
E-Spain
Tel.: (34) 944 79 43 74
Fax: (34) 944 79 43 83
E-Mail: information@osha.europa.eu
Homepage: www.europe.osha.europa.eu

Director
TAKALA, Jukka

European Maritime Safety Agency
12, rue de Genève
B-1140 Brussels
Homepage: www.emsa.europa.eu

Executive Director
DE RUITER, Willem

European Aviation Safety Authority
Ottoplatz, 1
D-50679 Koeln
Germany
Tel: +49 (0) 221 8999 0000
Fax: +49 (0) 221 8999 0999
E-Mail: info@easa.europa.eu
Homepage: www.easa.europa.eu

Executive Director
GOUDOU, Patrick

European Railway Agency
160, Boulevard Henri Harpignies
59300 Valenciennes – France
Telephone: ++33 327 096-500
Fax: +33 327 334-065
E-Mail: press-info@era.europa.eu
Internet: www.era.europa.eu

Director
VERSLYPE, Marcel

European Foundation for the Improvement of Living and Working Conditions
Wyattville Road
Loughlinstown
Dublin 18
Ireland
Tel.: (353-1) 204 31 00
Fax: (353-1) 282 64 56
E-Mail: postmaster@eurofound.europa.eu
Homepaget: www.eurofound.europa.eu

Director
KARPPINEN, Jorma

European Training Foundation
Villa Gualino
Viale Settimio Severo, 65
I-10133 Torino
Italy

Tel.: (39) 011 630 22 22
Fax: (39) 011 630 22 00
E-Mail: info@etf.europa.eu
Homepage: www.etf.europa.eu

Director
DUNBAR, Muriel

European Medicines Agency
7 Westferry Circus
Canary Wharf
London E14 4HB
United Kingdom
Tel.: (44-20) 74 18 84 00
Fax: (44-20) 74 18 84 16
E-Mail: mail@emea.europa.eu
Homepage: www.emea.europa.eu

Executive Director
LOENNGREN, Thomas

European Centre for Disease Prevention and Control
Tomtebodavaegen 11A
Solna, Sweden
Tel: +46(0)8 30 00 56
Fax: +46 (0)8 30 00 57
Homepage: www.ecdc.europa.eu

Director
JAKAB, Zsuzsanna

European Monitoring Centre for Drugs and Drug Addiction
Rua da Cruz de Santa
Apolónia, 23-25
1149-045 Lisboa
Portugal
Phone: (351-21) 811 30 00
Fax: (351-21) 813 17 11
E-Mail: info@emcdda.europa.eu
Hompage: www.emcdda.europa.eu

Director
GOETZ, Wolfgang

VI. European Institutions, Agencies and other bodies *(continued)*

Community Plant Variety Office
3, bd du Maréchal Foch
49000 Angers
France
Tel: (33) 241 25 64 00
Fax: (33) 241 25 64 10
E-Mail: cpvo@cpvo.europa.eu
Homepage: www.cpvo.europa.eu

President
KIEWIET, Bart

European Network and Information Security Agency
Vassilika Vouton
70013 Heraklion - Crete
Greece
Tel.: (30) 28 10 39 12 80
Fax: (30) 28 10 39 14 10
E-Mail: info@enisa.europa.eu
Internet: www.enisa.europa.eu

Executive Director
PIROTTI, Andrea

European Monitoring Centre on Racism and Xenophobia
Rahlgasse 3
1060 Wien
Austria
Tel.: (43-1) 580 30-0
Fax: (43-1) 580 30-99
E-Mail: office@eumc.europa.eu
Homepage: eumc.europa.eu

Director
WINKLER, Beate

Office for Official Publications of the European Communities
L-2985 Luxembourg
Tel: + 352 2929 2222
Fax: + 352 2929 42755
E-Mail: opoce-info-copyright@ec.europa.eu

General Director
CRANFIELD, Thomas

Group VII

History of the European Union

War and Peace

For centuries, Europe was the scene of frequent and bloody wars. Between 1870 and 1945, France and Germany fought each other three times, with terrible losses of life. A number of European leaders became convinced that the only way to secure a lasting peace between their countries was to unite them economically and politically.

So, in 1950, in a speech inspired by Jean Monnet, the French Foreign Minister Robert Schuman proposed integrating the coal and steel industries of Western Europe. As a result, the European Coal and Steel Community (ECSC) was established in 1951 with six members: Belgium, West Germany, Luxembourg, France, Italy and the Netherlands. The power to make decisions about the coal and steel industry in these countries was placed in the hands of an independent, supranational body called the "High Authority". Jean Monnet was its first President.

From three communities to the European Union

The ECSC was such a success that, within a few years, these same six countries decided to further integrate the other sectors of their economies. In 1957, they signed the Treaties of Rome, creating the European Atomic Energy Community (EURATOM) and the European Economic Community (EEC). The member states then set about removing trade barriers between them and forming a "common market".

In 1967, the institutions of the three European communities were merged. From this point on, there was a single Commission and a single Council of Ministers as well as the European Parliament.

Originally, the members of the European Parliament were chosen by the national parliaments, but in 1979, the first direct elections were held. Citizens of the member states were allowed to vote for the candidate of their choice. Since then, direct elections have been held every five years.

The Treaty of Maastricht (1992) introduced new forms of cooperation between the member state governments in the areas of defence and "justice and home affairs". With this system of inter-governmental cooperation, the Maastricht Treaty created the European Union (EU).

Integration means common policies

Economic and political integration between the member states of the European Union means that these countries have to take joint decisions on many matters. Thus, they have developed common policies in a very wide range of fields ranging from agriculture to culture, consumer affairs, competition, environment, energy, transport and trade.

In the early days, the focus was on a common commercial policy for coal and steel and a common agricultural policy. Other policies were added as when and the need arose. Some key policy aims have changed in the light of changing circumstances. For example, the aim of the agricultural policy is no longer to produce as much food as cheaply as possible but to support farming methods producing healthy, high-quality food while protecting the environment. The need for environmental protection is now taken into account across the whole range of EU policies.

The European Union's relations with the rest of the world have also become important. The EU negotiates major trade and aid agreements with other countries and is developing a Common Foreign and Security Policy.

The Single Market: banning the barriers

It took some time for the Member States to remove all the barriers to trade between them and to turn their "common market" into a genuine single market where goods, services, people and capital could move freely. Although the Single Market was formally completed at the end of 1992, there is still work to be done in some areas. There is still a real need to create a genuinely single market in financial services.

During the 1990s, it became increasingly easy for people to move around in Europe, as passport and customs checks were abolished at most of the EU's internal borders. One consequence is greater mobility for EU citizens. Since 1987, more than a million young Europeans have taken study courses abroad, with support from the EU.

The Single Currency: the euro in your pocket

In 1992, the EU decided to form an Economic and Monetary Union (EMU), involving the introduction of a single European currency managed by a European Central Bank. The single currency, the euro, became a reality on 1 January 2002, when euro notes and coins replaced national currencies in twelve of the 15 countries of the European Union (Belgium, Germany, Greece, Spain, France, Ireland, Italy, Luxembourg, the Netherlands, Austria, Portugal and Finland).

The growing family

The EU has grown in size with successive waves of accessions. Denmark, Ireland and the United Kingdom joined in 1973, followed by Greece in 1981, Spain and Portugal in 1986 and Austria, Finland and Sweden in 1995. The European Union welcomed ten new countries in 2004: Cyprus, the Czech Republic, Estonia, Hungary, Latvia, Lithuania, Malta, Poland, Slovakia and Slovenia. Bulgaria and Romania followed in 2007. Croatia is expected to be the next new member. Turkey has begun membership negotiations in 2005. A streamlined decision-making system is needed to ensure the continued efficiency of the enlarged EU. The Treaty of Nice—it came into force on 1 February 2003—sought to address these issues by laying down new rules on the size of the EU institutions and the way they work.

But nevertheless there was still a strong will among the peoples of Europe to formulate an European constitution. The fact that the elaboration of the constitution was entrusted to a Convention in which representatives of national parliaments, the European Parliament, the national governments and the Commission openly discussed the future of the Union has been one of the most outstanding developments of recent years. The result of these deliberations went beyond expectations. The Intergovernmental Conference that hat to give its final agreement has largely taken on board the Convention's proposals.

The Constitution, which was signed on 29 October 2004 and approved by the European Parliament on 12 January 2005, has to be ratified by each member state in accordance with its own constitutional requirements.

European Integration-Key Dates Events

Date	Event
May 9, 1950	Robert Schuman proposes pooling Europe's coal and steel industries.
April 18, 1951	European Coal and Steel Community (WCSC) Treaty signed in Paris.
March 25, 1957	European Economic Community (EEC) and European Atomic Energy Community (EURATOM) Treaties signed in Rome.
April 8, 1965	Treaty merging the institutions of the three European Communities signed.
July 1, 1968	Customs union completed
January 1, 1973	Denmark, Ireland and the United Kingdom join the Community.
March 13, 1979	European Monetary System (EMS) becomes operational.
January 1, 1981	Greece joins the European Community.
June 29, 1985	European Council endorses "White Paper" plan to complete single market by end 1992.
January 1, 1986	Spain and Portugal join the Community.
July 1, 1987	Single European Act (SEA) enters into force.
June 26–27, 1989	Madrid European Council endorses plan for Economic and Monetary Union (EMU).
October 3, 1990	The five federal states of the former German Democratic Republic enter the Community as part of a united Germany.
October 21, 1991	European Community and European Free Trade Association (EFTA) agree to form the European Economic Area (EEA).
December 11, 1991	Maastricht European Council agrees on Treaty on European Union.
December 16, 1991	Poland, Hungary, and Czechoslovakia sign first Europe Agreements on trade and political cooperation.
January 1, 1993	Establishment of European Single Market.
November 1, 1993	Treaty on European Union (Maastricht Treaty) enters into force
January 1, 1995	Austria, Finland, and Sweden join the European Union.
June 17, 1997	Treaty of Amsterdam is concluded.

Date	Event
March 12, 1998	European conference in London launches Europe-wide consultations on issues related to Common Foreign and Security Policy (CFSP) and Justice and Home Affairs (JHA).
March 30–31,1998	EU opens membership negotiations with Cyprus, Czech Republic, Estonia, Hungary, Poland, and Slovenia.
May 2, 1998	Eleven EU member states qualify to launch the euro on January 1, 1999.
June 1, 1998	European Central Bank (ECB) inaugurated in Frankfurt, Germany.
January 1, 1999	EMU and euro launched in eleven EU countries.
May 1, 1999	Treaty of Amsterdam enters into force.
December 1999	European Council meeting in Helsinki decides to open accession negotiations with Bulgaria, Latvia, Lithuania, Malta Romania, and the Slovak Republic and to recognize Turkey as a candidate country.
December 2000	European Council agrees on Treaty of Nice. EU leaders formally proclaim the Charter of Fundamental Rights of the European Union.
February 26, 2001	Regulation adopted establishing the Rapid Reaction Force.
January–February 2002	The Euro becomes legal tender and permanently replaces national currencies in EMU countries.
December 12–13, 2002	The European Council announces that Cyprus, Czech Republic, Estonia, Hungary, Latvia, Lithuania, Malta, Poland, Slovak Republic, and Slovenia will become EU members by May 1, 2004.
February 1, 2003	The Treaty of Nice enters into force.
April 16, 2003	Treaty of Accession (2003) is signed in Athens, Greece.
May 1, 2004	Cyprus, Czech Republic, Estonia, Hungary, Latvia, Lithuania, Malta, Poland, Slovak Republic, and Slovenia become EU Member States.
October 29, 2004	All Member States-Governments signed the Treaty establishing a Constitution for Europe. The Treaty has to be ratified in all Member States to enter in force. This process is still continuing.
January 1, 2007	Romania and Bulgaria joined the EU

Group VIII

Berlin Declaration of the 27 Member States of the European Union together with the European Parliament and European Commission on the Occasion of the Fiftieth Anniversary of the Signing Ceremony of the Treaties of Rome

Berlin, March 25, 2007

For centuries Europe has been an idea, holding out hope of peace and understanding. That hope has been fulfilled. European unification has made peace and prosperity possible. It has brought about a sense of community and overcome differences. Each Member State has helped to unite Europe and to strengthen democracy and the rule of law. Thanks to the yearning for freedom of the peoples of Central and Eastern Europe the unnatural division of Europe is now consigned to the past. European integration shows that we have learnt the painful lessons of a history marked by bloody conflict. Today we live together as was never possible before.

We, the citizens of the European Union, have united for the better.

I.

In the European Union, we are turning our common ideals into reality: for us, the individual is paramount. His dignity is inviolable. His rights are inalienable. Women and men enjoy equal rights. We are striving for peace and freedom, for democracy and the rule of law, for mutual respect and shared responsibility, for prosperity and security, for tolerance and participation, for justice and solidarity.

We have a unique way of living and working together in the European Union. This is expressed through the democratic interaction of the Member States and the European institutions. The European

Union is founded on equal rights and mutually supportive cooperation. This enables us to strike a fair balance between Member States' interests.

We preserve in the European Union the identities and diverse traditions of its Member States. We are enriched by open borders and a lively variety of languages, cultures and regions. There are many goals which we cannot achieve on our own, but only in concert. Tasks are shared between the European Union, the Member States and their regions and local authorities.

II.

We are facing major challenges which do not stop at national borders. The European Union is our response to these challenges. Only together can we continue to preserve our ideal of European society in future for the good of all European Union citizens. This European model combines economic success and social responsibility. The common market and the euro make us strong. We can thus shape the increasing interdependence of the global economy and ever-growing competition on international markets according to our values. Europe's wealth lies in the knowledge and ability of its people; that is the key to growth, employment and social cohesion.

We will fight terrorism, organised crime and illegal immigration together. We stand up for liberties and civil rights also in the struggle against those who oppose them. Racism and xenophobia must never again be given any rein.

We are committed to the peaceful resolution of conflicts in the world and to ensuring that people do not become victims of war, terrorism and violence. The European Union wants to promote freedom and development in the world. We want to drive back poverty, hunger and disease. We want to continue to take a leading role in that fight.

We intend jointly to lead the way in energy policy and climate protection and make our contribution to averting the global threat of climate change.

III.

The European Union will continue to thrive both on openness and on the will of its Member States to consolidate the Union's internal development. The European Union will continue to promote democracy, stability and prosperity beyond its borders.

With European unification a dream of earlier generations has become a reality. Our history reminds us that we must protect this for the good of future generations. For that reason we must always renew the political shape of Europe in keeping with the times. That is why today, 50 years after the signing of the Treaties of Rome, we are united in our aim of placing the European Union on a renewed common basis before the European Parliament elections in 2009.

For we know, Europe is our common future.

EU leaders signing the Berlin Declaration

The Berlin Declaration of the European Union, March 25, 2007

EU leaders before the Brandenburg Gate, March 25, 2007

Chancellor Merkel and EU leaders

About the Authors

José Manuel Barroso has been the President of the European Commission since 2004. From 1999 until 2002, he was Vice President of the European People's Party and Vice President of the Center Democrats International. Mr Barroso has also been a member of various informal advisory groups to the Secretary General of the United Nations, including the Secretary General's Resource Group on the Democratic Republic of Congo. He was an elected member of the Portuguese parliament six times consecutively since 1985, was Chairman of the Portuguese Parliament's Foreign Affairs Committee between 1995 and 1996, acted as State Secretary for Home Affairs and for Foreign Affairs and Cooperation and Minister for Foreign Affairs. He was Prime Minister of Portugal from 2002 to 2004.

Mr. Barroso holds a law degree from the University of Lisbon, a Master's degree in Political Science and a Diploma in European Studies, both with honors, from the University of Geneva. He also studied at Columbia University, Georgetown University, the International University Institute in Luxembourg, and the European University Institute in Florence. He was a visiting professor at Georgetown University from 1996 to 1998 and head of the International Relations Department at Lusíada University from 1995 to 1999. Mr. Barroso has held various scholarships, including from the Swiss Confederation, the Commission of the European Communities, the Volkswagenwerk Foundation, NATO and the Swiss National Fund for Scientific Research.

Elmar Brok has been a member of the European Parliament since 1980. He is a member of the board of the European People's Party and European Democrats Group (EPP-ED) and also a member of the Committee on Foreign Affairs, and the delegation for relations with the United States. He was chairman of the Committee on Foreign Affairs from 2000 to 2007. He acted as the parliament's representative at the Intergovernmental Conference in Amsterdam in 1996/97 and at Nice in 2000, as its representative in the Council's Reflection Group preparing for the reform of the Maastricht Treaty, as Reporter in Chief on the Enlargement (1999–2004), as representative at the intergovernmental conference for the EU Constitutional Treaty

(2003/2004), and as EPP Coordinator in the EU Constitutional Convention. He studied Law and Political Science at the Center of European Governmental Studies at the University of Edinburgh. From 1999 to 2006 he was President of *Europa-Union Deutschland*. He has served as deputy chairman of the *Europäische Bewegung Deutschlands*, deputy chairman of the Transatlantic Policy Network Parliamentary Group, co-chairman of the Transatlantic Legislators' Dialogue, and deputy member of the Committee on European Union Affairs in the German Bundestag.

Benita Ferrero-Waldner has been Commissioner for External Relations of the European Union since December 2004. From 2000 to 2004, she was the first female Federal Minister for Foreign Affairs of the Republic of Austria, and in 1995 she became the first female State Secretary in that ministry. In 1994, Dr. Ferrero-Waldner acted as Chief of Protocol of the United Nations in the Executive Office of UN Secretary General Boutros Boutros-Ghali. Prior to this position, she served as an Austrian foreign service officer in Madrid, Dakar, and Paris, and as Deputy Chief of Protocol in the Austrian Ministry for Foreign Affairs. Before joining the ministry, Dr. Ferrero-Waldner worked in the private sector, mostly in Germany. She studied law in Salzburg.

Falk-Ulrich von Hoff was counsellor of the EPP-ED-Group of the European Parliament in Brussels, Berlin and Strasbourg and secretary general of the CDU-CSU delegation to the European Parliament from 1988 to 2004. From 1982 to 1988, he acted as head of the European office of the CDU-CSU group of the German Bundestag, prior to which he was a civil servant in the Ministry of the Interior of the state of Schleswig-Holstein and Representative of the Konrad Adenauer Foundation in Lima, Peru. He also practiced law in Hamburg and worked as assistant to German MP Dr. Günther Rinsche in Bonn. He studied law at the Universities of Bonn, Hamburg and Göttingen and received his doctorate in 1974.

Werner Langen is a member of the European Parliament and a member of the bureau of the Group of the European People's Party (Christian Democrats) and European Democrats. He is chairman of the German Delegation in the EPP-ED-Group and a member of the Committee on Industry, Research and Energy and the Delegation to the EU-Turkey Joint Parliamentary Committee. He was parliamentary director of the CDU/CSU-Group in the European Parliament (1999–2006), chairman of the CDU in Rheinland-Palatinate (1992–1993), Minister for Agricultural Affairs in Rheinland-Palatinate, Chairman of the Agricultural Committee of the Federal Council of Germany (1990–1991), and member of the state parliament of Rhineland-Palatinate (1983–1994). He received an advanced degree in economics and doctorate in political economy from the University of Bonn/University of Cologne.

Angela Merkel was sworn in as Chancellor of the Federal Republic of Germany on November 22, 2005. She is the first woman and the first east German to hold this office. She has also chaired the Christian Democratic Union Germany (CDU) since 2000. Between 2002-2005 she was Chair of the CDU/CSU parliamentary group in the German Bundestag, and between 1998-2000 General Secretary of the CDU. Between 1994-1998 she served as Federal Minister for the Environment, Nature Conservation and Nuclear Safety; and from 1991 – 1994 as Federal Minister for Women and Youth. She has been a member of the German Bundestag since 1990. During the tumultuous events in east Germany in 1989 she became a member of the opposition party Demokratischer Aufbruch (Democratic Awakening) and in 1990 joined the CDU. During that year she was Deputy Government Spokeswoman of the freely elected east German government under Lothar de Maizière. She was awarded a doctorate in 1986 and between 1978 and 1990 she was a member of the academic staff at the Central Institute of Physical Chemistry at the Academy of Sciences. Between 1973 and 1978 she studied physics at Leipzig University.

Hartmut Nassauer is Member of the European Parliament; Vice-President of the Group of the European People's Party (Christian Democrats) and European Democrats (EPP-ED-Group); and Chairman of the Delegation for relations with the countries of Southeast Asia and the Association of Southeast Asian Nations (ASEAN).

Doris Pack is a member of the Bureau of the Group of the European People's Party (Christian Democrats) and European Democrats, chairwoman of the Delegation for Relations with the Countries of Southeast Europe, and member of the European Parliament's Conference of Delegation Chairmen, the Committee on Culture and Education, and the Committee on Women's Rights and Gender Equality. She is president of Women in the EPP and executive member of the

European People's Party (EPP), vice president of the European Cultural Foundation Germany ECF/D, president of the Open University Association (VHS Saar), vice president of the European Movement Saar and member of the ZDF Television Council. She also presides over the foundation for German/French cultural relations and the European children and youth book fair in the Saarland. She has been a member of the European Parliament since 1989. In the past, she was a Member of various city councils and a member of the Bundestag from 1974 to 1983 and from 1985 to 1989. In addition, she was a member of the Parliamentary Assembly of the Council of Europe and of the WEU Assembly from 1981 to 1983 and from 1985 to 1989. She graduated from teaching college and taught in primary schools before working for the Saarland Ministry of Education from 1983 to 1985.

Hans-Gert Poettering has been chairman of the Group of the European People's Party (Christian Democrats) and European Democrats of the European People's Party in the European Parliament since 1999. He is a member of the Conference of Presidents and of the Committee on Constitutional Affairs. He was president of *Europa-Union Deutschland* from 1997 to 1999 and head of the CDU list for Germany and Lower Saxony for the 2004 European Parliament elections. From 1981 to 1991, he acted as chairman of the Lower Saxony *Europa-Union*, has been chairman of the Osnabrück district CDU since 1990, and acted as European affairs spokesman of the Junge Union of Lower Saxony from 1974 to 1980. He studied law, political science, and history at the University of Bonn and the Institut des Hautes Etudes Internationales in Geneva. In addition, he studied at Columbia University and received his doctorate in law in 1974.

Günter Rinsche was president of the Konrad-Adenauer-Foundation from 1995 to 2001. As a member of the European Parliament from 1979 to 1999, he acted as president of the EP-Conference of Delegation Chairmen, chairman of the CDU/CSU-Group in the EP, member of the EP Committee of Foreign Affairs, and president of the EP-Delegation for ASEAN, Southeast Asia and South Korea. He was a member of the state legislature of North Rhine-Westphalia from 1975 to 1980 and the economic spokesman of his party. While serving in the German Bundestag, he also acted as deputy chairman of the Committee for Economic Cooperation (Development Policy). From 1964 to 1979, Dr. Rinsche was lord mayor of the city of Hamm.

He studied economics and political science at the universities of Münster and Cologne and was a Fulbright scholar at Colorado College, Colorado Springs. He received his doctorate in economics in 1959 and has published more than 25 books.

Bernhard Vogel has been chairman of the Konrad-Adenauer-Foundation since 2001. From 1992 to 2003, he was prime minister of the state of Thuringia, and from 1976 to 1988, he held the same post in the state of Rhineland-Palatinate. He was speaker of the Upper House of the German Parliament (*Bundesrat*) in 1987-88 and representative for Cultural Affairs of the Federal Republic of Germany within the framework of the Agreement on German-French Cooperation from 1979 to 1982. He has been a member of the Federal Council of the CDU since 1975 and party chairman of the CDU in the State of Rhineland-Palatinate from 1974 to 1988. From 1971 to 1988, he was a member of parliament of the state of Rhineland-Palatinate, from 1967 to 1976, he was Minister for Education and Culture of the state of Rhineland-Palatinate, and from 1965 to 1967, he served as a member of the German Bundestag. He studied political science, history, sociology and economics at the universities of Heidelberg and Munich and was awarded his doctorate in 1960. He has received numerous honorary doctorates, among others from the Catholic University of America, the University of Lublin, and the German College for Administrative Sciences in Speyer. In 2003, he was awarded an honorary professorial degree by the prime minister of the State of Baden-Württemberg.

Norbert Wagner has been director of the Konrad Adenauer Foundation (KAS) in Washington, D.C. since 2005. From 1996 to 2004, he was director of the Paris office of the Konrad Adenauer Foundation, covering France and Italy. In 1990 he founded the Moscow office of the KAS and served as its director between 1990 and 1995. From 1987 to 1990, he was advisor at the Institute of Southeast Asian Studies in Singapore and the representative of the Konrad Adenauer Foundation in Singapore. In 1986-87 he was a visiting fellow at Yale University's Economic Growth Center, and from 1975 to 1986 he was assistant professor at Heidelberg University, lecturing on international economics and development economics. He received his doctorate and master's degree in Economics from Heidelberg University.

Gerhard Wahlers has been the head of the International Division of the Konrad Adenauer Foundation in Berlin since 2003. Prior to this position, he was the head of the KAS office in Washington, D.C. and in Jerusalem. He joined the Konrad Adenauer Foundation as an advisor in the International Cooperation Division in 1990. He studied social sciences and history (for high school teaching) at the University of Münster. He also studied history, sociology, and political science and conducted research studies in Venezuela, Columbia, the Dominican Republic, Chile, Argentina, and Brazil. He received his doctorate in philosophy from the University of Münster.

Karl von Wogau is chairman of the Subcommittee on Security and Defense in the European Parliament. He is a member of the Bureau of the Group of the European People's Party (Christian Democrats) and European Democrats, a member of the Committee on Foreign Affairs and the delegation for relations with the NATO Parliamentary Assembly. He was a member of the Federal Executive Committee of the CDU/CSU Small Business Association from 1983 to 1989 and held a managerial post in a large firm in Basel from 1971 to 1984. He studied law and received a doctorate from INSEAD in 1973.